THIS IS NO BOOK
A Gay Reader

Gregory Woods

For Rosie –
with fab kisses, etc.

Mushroom 5/12/94

love,
Greg

mushroom
P·U·B·L·I·C·A·T·I·O·N·S

This Is No Book
A Gay Reader

Published in 1994 by Mushroom Publications
10–12 Heathcote St., Nottingham NG1 3AA

Printed in Great Britain by Antony Rowe

ISBN 0907123260

Camerado, this is no book,
Who touches this touches a man.

(Walt Whitman)

ACKNOWLEDGEMENTS

*These review essays were first published
in the following journals:*

*European Gay Review, Frontiers,
Gay's the Word Review,
Lesbian and Gay Socialist,
New Statesman, Rouge,
Times Literary Supplement
and Word and Image.*

CONTENTS

CONTENTS

THE MAKING OF A GAY READER

How do you become a gay reader? What does gay reading involve? We are often told that many lesbians and gay men — mainly those who do not come out when they first find out that they are gay, and who therefore do not have suitable friends to talk to — come to terms with their discovered sexuality by reading books. It may be that by reading you learn that you are not the only queer on the planet; or that there are hostile strangers who wish you dead; or even that you will, after all, be able to work out a way of living your life as you choose. Your development may be marked as much by encounters with particular texts as by conversations or physical events. Certainly, in the nineteen-sixties, when I grew up, books gave me what television did not. I constructed my identity as a gay man by reading fiction before I actually met and made love with other gay men. I was amazed by Plato's *Symposium* long before I witnessed the simple fact of two men kissing.

In 1966 I had been sent to a minor Catholic public school, because my father, uncle and elder brother had all been there before me. Notorious as 'hotbeds' of homosexuality, the English public schools had prepared generations of adolescents for the rigours of imperial life by policing them with Greek and Latin, rugby football, beatings, cold baths and casual brutality. We boys knew the rumours about single-sex boarding schools, and many did their best to live up to them. All our gossip was about each other's relationships. It was assumed we could discreetly do more or less as we liked for the time being, so long as we had stopped being queer when we left. But it was those of us who believed we would not become heterosexual, who had the least relaxed time of it. What with all the fear and guilt, our beds were rarely hot.

We watched the distant outside world with interest. The passing of the 1967 Sexual Offences Act partially decriminalized sex between men over 21. We read the small-ads in *Oz* and *International Times* and dreamed of daring to reply to them. We learned the new use of the word 'gay'. But, notwithstanding the theoretical platonism of our environment, we were closely policed. In my final year, while looking through the files of the school's Law Society, I found a letter from the Homosexual Law Reform Society. It was a brief expression of regret, that the school group had been forced to withdraw its invitation to a speaker. No other outside speaker — humanist or communist or whatever — had ever been vetoed.

It occurred to me that, without ignoring or going against what I had been taught, my best strategy for exam-passing was to concentrate on subjects that interested me. So for my History of Art A-level, which I sat in 1970, I wrote a dissertation on Donatello and an essay on David Hockney. In both, I tackled the question of sexuality, if not head-on, at least in the oblique manner that I judged to be expedient. When it came to English, I found myself writing an essay on Hamlet's relationship with Horatio. Apparently, I had already learnt (but not actually been taught) the limits of academic openness: for, although my essay proposed a homosexual relationship, my concluding paragraph coolly dismissed the very idea. The fact that I still remember doing this suggests how intensely I felt both the need to write about such things and the unstated pressure not to.

Before leaving school I had read what now seems to me quite an impressive array of gay literature, from Peter Whigham's translations of Catullus to Mann's *Death in Venice*, Plato's *Symposium* to Baldwin's *Giovanni's Room* and *Another Country*. I had found Thom Gunn's *The Sense of Movement* in the school library, and drawn my own conclusions about its 'hidden' meanings. Already a compulsive browser in second-hand bookshops, I had mustered a small collection of contemporary gay fiction, both English and American. This post-adolescent enthusiasm was no mere search for texts to masturbate to. It was that, too, of course; but it was part of the re-shaping of my personality that followed the physical tranformations of puberty. It also laid the foundation for all my subsequent scholarship. But what strikes me as most interesting from my present perspective is that, although I was in the middle of one of the most expensive and elitist educations on offer anywhere in the world, as a gay man I was an autodidact. All of my gay cultural knowledge was self-taught.

In 1971 I went to one of Britain's new, purpose-built universities, which prided themselves on their modernity and progressiveness. In my first week as an undergraduate, during a seminar on W.H. Auden's poem 'Lay your sleeping head, my love,' we spoke of the poem's addressee as 'she' throughout the first hour of our discussion. Finally, our tutor told us Auden was homosexual. Did this information, he asked, change the meaning of the poem? True to the liberalism expected of our generation, we decided at once that there was no significant, qualitative difference between homosexual and heterosexual love, and none, therefore, between the love poems each might produce. We handled the knowledge that Auden was gay, in other words, by denying that it mattered he was gay. I doubted our argument, and went back to my room feeling that the issue had not been faced. But I was not equipped, with either confidence or evidence, to have argued the contrary view.

The following year, I attended a seminar on Allen Ginsberg's 'America', chaired by a young, male lecturer with long hair and fashionable earrings. When asked if the poet was homosexual, he felt it was appropriate to reply, 'Oh yes, he's as queer as a coot!' Students giggled. After more than twenty years, I can still hear his tone, see his face, and feel my own discomfort. The statement, while superficially acknowledging the sexual issue, was in fact a clear signal that the subject was to be dismissed from any serious level of discussion. After all, weren't we all adults — too sophisticated to make an issue of it? Compliant as ever, we let the matter drop.

In my final year as an undergraduate, I went to a seminar on *A Passage to India*. The lecturer, a socialist, asked me a complicated question about the politics of the book. I replied that E.M. Forster's obvious, but still covert, erotic interest in the untouchable youth in the courtroom scenes undermined, or even invalidated, whatever other social point he was trying to make. Unless we confronted the author's homosexuality, I argued, we could not come to any serious conclusion about the totality of his political views. Still in the closet at the time, I was embarrassed to have brought up the subject — it still made me blush — but quite proud to have done so without being struck by lightning. Far from taking my point, the lecturer accused me of not listening to what was being said in class. The question was repeated for me, in an angry tone, in much the same words as the first time, but as slowly and 'patiently' as though I were an idiot. Angry at being humiliated in this way, I repeated my original reply at the same sarcastic, slow pace. My point was ignored. The politics question was put to another student, and the discussion went off in the direction our tutor had preordained.

Somehow undiscouraged, I eventually registered to write a Ph.D. thesis on gay men's poetry. In the years that followed it was always made clear to me, by implication, that my research would have to be both broader and more detailed than in any comparable thesis on a more 'respectable' topic. What was also clear was that I needed a more receptive audience for my work than was available even in a progressive academic department.

So in the late nineteen-seventies I began reviewing books for Alison Hennegan at *Gay News*. Literary journalism was my way of combining my roles as a scholar and an activist. It remains so today. Whether I write for gay newspapers or predominantly straight cultural journals, I have — to use a dated phrase — gay liberationist aims. The same goes for my work as a university lecturer.

While teaching at a university in southern Italy in 1984, I decided to give a series of unpaid public lectures on homosexuality and English literature. The series was advertised in the Italian gay press. Days before the first lecture, my professor — a communist, who sincerely believed himself committed to *la lotta*, the 'struggle' — forced me to add the following note to all publicity material: 'These lectures have no relation to the English language and literature courses in Professor X's department'.

In 1986, chairing an undergraduate seminar on Auden's 'Lay your sleeping head, my love,' I withheld the information that the poet was gay until half an hour's discussion of his attitude to his 'girlfriend' had taken place. When I asked 'If I told you he was homosexual, would you read it differently?' I heard exactly the same answers which we had given to the same question when I was a student. Nothing, it seemed, had changed.

In April 1989 I attended an interview for an academic post at a northern university. Two questions I was asked were not unexpected: Was Shakespeare a homosexual? Is E.M. Forster's *Maurice* a good book? This was the first interview at which I had to answer both. If you want to survive you are expected to answer 'No' to both. This is easy enough in the case of Shakespeare, since there was no concept of 'a homosexual' in his time. But I am not certain I agree with all of Forster's detractors, many of them motivated by homophobia, that *Maurice* is so awful. Precisely because of its uneasy commitment to important social issues, I rather like it. It may be a botched job, but that is by no means only Forster's fault.

In July 1989 I attended a meeting of A-level examiners in a London hotel. At lunch I sat opposite the most friendly and approachable of my fellow examiners, a middle-aged woman, who had shown in the meeting a range of humane and liberal attitudes to the students whose work we were reading, and a generous approach to assessment. Half-way through the meal, she asked about my SILENCE = DEATH lapel button. When I told her it was a slogan from the AIDS crisis, she asked in apparently genuine bewilderment, 'Why are you interested in *that?*'

One of the outcomes of my search for gay readings has been that I am often accused of 'reading things into' books in which those 'things' did not previously exist: sexual things into innocent contexts, queer things into straight texts. Gay readings are said to spoil books, whereas censorious straight readings are considered 'universal' and, therefore, more than adequate to the requirements of any but the most filthy-minded of readers. When Jeffrey Meyers reviewed *Articulate Flesh*, my book about gay men's poetry, his fiercest criticism of it was that it was 'primarily intended . . . for a homosexual audience' and that it was consequently 'unlikely to convince an objective reader'. This contrast between the lordly objectivity of heterosexual readings (that is, of readings which distance themselves from, or even obliterate, a text's gay meanings) and the sordid subjectivity of gay readings is ignorant drivel. But it is the prevailing view. In exactly the same way, our culture still values white readers over black, and male over female. In such a situation, reading itself inevitably becomes a dissident act, however modest.

The title of this book comes from 'So Long', a poem in which Walt Whitman identifies his physical life so closely with his poetry that he admits no distinction between the two. He writes:

> Camerado, this is no book,
> Who touches this touches a man.

While not all readers are pleased to be caught holding the poet's body in their laps, Whitman's stategy of implicating his readers in his own sex life — or in his written fantasies, at least — is seriously meant as a plea that the barriers between literature and social life should be collapsed. That is why I have chosen to quote him here. Very little gay literature is escapist. We read texts — even our science fiction, pornography or romance — which deal with the realities of identities either imposed on or created by us. We read about the situations into which our bodies place us, and the positions into which we put our bodies. While you can't catch a virus from a book (although William Burroughs might argue otherwise) you can learn about the health care, political resistance and safer sexual strategies about which straight writers are so often so ignorant or, worse still, so culpably misleading. Whether you live in the remote countryside or in crowded inner-city alienation, gay readings can turn your solitude into solidarity. Few texts could have a nobler purpose than this.

ORDINARY BOYHOOD

Wilhelm von Gloeden, *Taormina* (London: Gay Men's Press, 1984)

Anyone who doubts the magnificence of Wilhelm von Gloeden's photographs of Sicilian youths should look at them next to a copy of *Playgirl*. All those flawless American starlets, rendered terminally insipid by nature's own 'perfecting' airbrush, flaunting circumcisions as proof of their Upward Mobility, seem to me as bland as the cars or sofas they adorn. How I long for Duane Michals to undermine them with a facetious and misspelt caption, or for George Dureau to saw off their legs. God save me from men who sweat cologne!

My reaction to von Gloeden's boys depends on this contrast. I observe the variety of their foreskinned penises and the fact that their groins are tanned — no phantom shapes of shorts or briefs to turn the skin itself into a fetish. I note von Gloeden's impartial interest in both frontal and rear views, and I applaud his fascination with armpits.

It is ultimately, though, to the boys' extremities that I return most often — to the parts which would have been visible even if they had kept their clothes on: their faces, their feet and their hands, in that order. It is here that I locate the full charge of their attraction.

That any one of their faces is in a conventional sense beautiful — or 'handsome' as inhibited heterosexuals would have it — is sheer luck. It is only by chance, rather than by an act of selection on the photographer's part, that a strikingly pretty face appears among the rather plain and awkward faces of ordinary boyhood. This is a moral and aesthetic distinguishing feature of von Gloeden's work, which sets it apart from any form of pornography known to me. Only their characteristic thick-headedness made the Fascists destroy so many of the original plates.

Von Gloeden idolises — that is to say, he transforms into idols — even conventionally 'ugly' boys, because he believes, and it is the purpose of his work to show, that it is *boyhood* itself that is the height of beauty. The same applies to girlhood in his less numerous pictures of plain and pretty girls (none of which appears here).

I regret that there are few good shots of hands in this selection. In other photos one can often see dirt beneath the cracked nails and blisters on the palms, denoting labour. Similarly, the soles of the feet are crusty, the toes fat; these are the kinds of feet that reek, not of rubber and nylon, but of the earth. Emmanuel Cooper is right to mention Caravaggio in his introduction; like these boys, Caravaggio's angels have hands and feet which betray their earthly origins.

One should not, perhaps, speak of the soil of Taormina as though it were an English village. From the ruined castle at 1300 feet down to the shingle at Isola Bella, from the view of Calabria in the north to Etna in the south, this town deserves more than most to be used as a backdrop by photographers, whether tourists or professionals. (Von Gloeden was both.) So, my favourite image in the collection is of a boy reclining on a low wall, with Taormina reclining down his hip and thigh. They are literally part of each other.

Packed in summer with pairs of northern European clones, the town has not forgotten its debt to the eccentric Baron von Gloeden, and it is not embarrassed by him. 'He was the first tourist,' a shopkeeper there told me last year, 'we owe everything to him.' She spoke of him with real warmth as she led me by the hand to show me the villa he used to live in. The best restaurant in Taormina has framed enlargements of his photos all round its walls, and the food is served by boys with work-worn hands.

POLITICS OF JOY

Edward Carpenter, *Towards Democracy* (London: GMP, 1985)

'In 1883 he became a socialist and wrote *Towards Democracy*.'
This oddly dramatic account of the genesis of Carpenter's book
(from the Everyman *Dictionary of Literary Biography*) overlooks
the fact that its four sections were published in 1883, 1885, 1892
and 1902. The whole work, a massive millenarian sequence of
poems, was the product not of sudden conversion but of a life-style
conscientiously developed over decades.

Of course, Carpenter is easy to dismiss. His political vision,
expressed in terms more of joy than of economics, shrugs off the
practical details of how a state should be run: 'Stronger than all
the combinations of Capital, wiser than all the Committees
representative of Labor, the simple need and hunger of the
human heart. / Nothing more is needed.' And these opinions are
stated in poems which, at their worst, sound like a fumbling
intercourse between Whitman and McGonagall.

The book's mood ranges from gentle prettifications of the
British landscape and people to the kind of choking fury that
reappears later in D.H. Lawrence. When Carpenter calls England
'a dead waste of aimless abject closeshaven shabby simpering
flat pompous peaked punctilious faces,' we have to agree with
Emile Delavenay's argument (largely based on circumstantial
evidence) that this is one of Lawrence's main sources.

In addition to his ideological beard and tan, Carpenter shares
with Lawrence a tendency to become so involved in what he
wants to say, rather than in how he wants to say it, that only
enthusiasm is left to save him from his frequently deficient
diction. But there is no point in sneering when, for example, he
says life is 'a mere empty blob without Freedom'. The phrase is
ridiculous, but perfectly expressive of a ridiculous condition.

This apparent lack of sophistication can be a real virtue. I
believe that 'A Mightier Than Mammon', which is a folly built
on errors and contains some of the sloppiest writing in the book,
is, nevertheless, outstanding among English political poems. This
is partly because its message takes precedence over its rhetoric,
leaving the reader with an uncommon impression of sincerity.

It is also because the message, although simple and obvious,
is as devastating a threat — and as radical a solution — to the

condition of British society (then and now) as is the idea it complements, that the workers of the world should unite. Without new attitudes to sex, particularly to contraception and homosexuality, the redistribution of capital can have only superficial effects on the structure of society. Socialism depends on the realignment of the sexes.

Our century has not necessarily eased the process. When Carpenter personifies Democracy as a male lover poised to impregnate the female nation with freedom, the idea is not as sexist as it sounds: for he assumes we can imagine a phallus potent not with power and lust, but with humility and love. This requires a suspension of both sexual and political disbelief. After all, women and men alike, we under the Conservatives have a very different impression of how it feels to be fucked by Democracy.

That the published ideas of a Victorian ex-clergyman could be so far in advance of our own times, is worth remembering. *Towards Democracy* really earns its status as a Gay Modern Classic; but, like so many gay classics, it addresses itself as eloquently to the heterosexual hegemony as to those of us who are gay. In the end, it is to all of us that Carpenter directs his totally convincing view of Britain: 'I see a great land waiting for its own people to come and take possession of it'.

DIFFERENCES

Derek Jarman, *Caravaggio* (London: Thames & Hudson, 1986)

Caravaggio's paintings rely on a kind of irony that is common in gay poetry. It is an irony created by perfect balance between the 'neutral' and gay meanings of a text — a *double entendre*, the two meanings of which are not hierarchic (with the polite raised above the impolite), but which share power as equals. There is no hidden subtext; there is, rather, a suggestiveness that is quite open — if only to the suggestible.

Wittgenstein's diagram of the duck-rabbit works in a similar way. It depicts not a duck or a rabbit, but both at once or in rapid alternation. If you can see only one of them, you are not seeing the diagram at all.

So in Caravaggio's images the irony exists in the coincidence of two overt meanings. Indeed, each picture has two subjects: title and sitter. The two can no more be separated than (say) form and content in a Henry Moore; yet they are as distinctly separable as John the Baptist and a rent boy. You have not seen the painting until you have seen both of its images, sacred and profane, and registered the shock of that alternation between them: duck/rabbit/duck/rabbit/duck . . . Neither can be ignored.

The problem with Caravaggio is that his irony has been dulled by history. What was shocking when his works were first painted was as much their murkiness and their use of ordinary people in sacred roles as their occasional sexiness. Since cinema alone has accustomed us to all these things, we can no longer *see* Caravaggio's profanity, even if we can begin to imagine it.

Perhaps the only people who really saw the paintings as Caravaggio meant them to be seen were those sensitive clerics who banned them from their walls. The seers were those whose dull Faith made them refuse to see. (Similarly, the ideal viewers of Jarman's *Jubilee* would seem to be those who are too horrified by its violence to watch it.)

This brings me to what I think are the two main flaws in Jarman's brilliant, dislocated film, *Caravaggio:* it lacks anything as truly shocking as the paintings were in their day; and it lacks any of those simple believers who would have been the most shocked. (There are, frankly, too many gay priests here.)

The first defect was forced on Jarman. As he explains in the notes to his script, he had wanted to film the painting of 'Profane Love', but found that Equity does not provide cheerful little boys to flaunt the baldness of their balls. So the one painting that might still affect us as the artist would have wished — a naked child happily and knowingly impersonating the erotic Eros — is literally emasculated: Jarman cast Dawn Archibald in the role and kept her fully clothed.

The film's reconstructions of paintings are triumphs of approximation. None of them is an exact replica; indeed, their power depends to some extent on their *differences* from the originals — above all, on the slight movements of the posed actors: a blink, a twitch, a faltering hand. So I am not excited by Gerald Incandela's stills of them, but the rest of his photos, seen together with Jarman's notes and script, give a vivid, atmospheric account of work in progress. This is the book, not of the film, but of its filming. Glossiness apart, it is not finished.

The script includes chunks of superfluous voice-over narrative, much of which, mercifully, did not survive as far as the film. Its presence here reminds us that, when it comes to a choice between verbal and visual means, Jarman is always safer with the latter. So, if your finances force a choice on you too, rather than buy this somewhat purposeless book, go to see the film three times.

Then check out the National Gallery's newly acquired painting, Caravaggio's 'Boy Bitten by a Lizard'. It's a Freudian nightmare. But where the Viennese quack would be tossing in his sleep, you may well find a productive dream.

GAY AND GAY

Langston Hughes, *Selected Poems* (London: Pluto Press, 1986)

The poems in this selection are songs as much as poems. For
them to work on the cold page, you must read them slowly (don't
skim, because some of them are so short you'll hardly notice
you've read them) and you must allow your imagination to flesh
them out with a saxophone and a sensuous voice. Put on some
jazz; read Hughes out loud, but not in a monotone: try to sing
him, off key but with feeling, as a drunk might on a muggy
Harlem night.

Contrary to their appearance in print, his vowels do not have
measured, stable values: some must be wailed at leisure, for as
long as a trumpeter's breath might hold out; others get docked
to less than a syllable. These are not winter poems, countryside
poems or — although some deal with loneliness — solitude poems.
Imagine yourself reciting them in bed to an intimate stranger,
with the windows open, a cat howling on the fire escape, and a
couple rehearsing murder in the next room.

Langston Hughes (1902-1967) was the archetypal 'New
Negro' of the Harlem Renaissance period. He rejected the discreet
role that was required of him by whites and acquiescent blacks
(to whom Jazz and Blues were a lively embarrassment). He was
interested less in 'fine art' than in popular culture. A life-long
commitment to freedom and democracy of a kind somewhat more
humane than the 'democracy' and 'freedom' advocated by the
House Un-American Activities Committee made him, in the
Fifties, one of the two most popular of all black American
intellectuals (the other being Gwendolyn Brooks).

It may be that Hughes' poetic subjects now seem predictable,
especially if one is familiar with Blues lyrics: poverty, violence,
crime, abandoned women, Jim Crow and Uncle Tom; above all,
death and love, love and sex, sex and death. (But isn't imaginative
predictability one of the requirements of a popular art?) He speaks
with persuasive simplicity and humour, especially when outlining
his dreams of communion in community. It is always good to see
him quoting Jefferson and Lincoln to his American audience,
white and black alike: for to Hughes, 'America is a dream' —
but a dream deferred.

He is currently being celebrated as a central figure in the reassertion of gay pride in black communities on both sides of the Atlantic. This revival is only to be welcomed. But I think it is worth remembering that he identified principally as black rather than bisexual or gay. In this respect he is to be distinguished from more outspoken figures like Richard Bruce Nugent. Nugent, who was a friend, did not think of him as being gay; indeed, he said Hughes was 'asexual'.

The question of how many of the poems are 'gay poems' depends on how generous you are willing to be with regard to gender transposition. Given their origin in the drag-queen-filled basement clubs of Harlem, I find it hard to doubt that many of the 'women' referred to in the poems are men; and some of the 'men' are dykes. Furthermore, whenever Hughes uses the word 'gay' you can be sure he uses it, as early as 60 years ago, in both its main senses, meaning both happy and homosexual. (The use of the word in 'Water-Front Streets', one of my favourite gay and gay poems, is a good example.)

Hughes also has a very cute way of apparently heterosexualising a gay message. Look, for instance, at 'Joy', where the emotion joy is personified as a woman, but the real source of Joy's joy is emphatically male: 'I went to look for Joy, / Slim, dancing Joy, / Gay, laughing Joy, / Bright-eyed Joy — / And I found her / Driving the butcher's cart / In the arms of the butcher boy! / Such company, such company, / As keeps this young nymph, Joy!'

Most of his best love poems rely, like this, on an ironic interplay between a possible heterosexual and a probable homosexual version. Some of them are, quite conventionally, spoken by fictional female voices to male lovers. But even so, there is no mistaking the real meanings of a poem ('Port Town') that begins with the lines:

Hello, sailor boy,
In from the sea!
Hello, sailor,
Come with me!

If there is a hidden gay meaning here, it is as well hidden as a hard-on in a wet jockstrap. If not quite as pretty.

MONUMENT TO HOMOPHOBIA

Enzo Siciliano, *Pasolini* (London: Bloomsbury, 1987)

'Let Catholics beware of carrying the Trojan horse of Pasolini into the city of God'. This attack on Pasolini — launched by the lawyer who was prosecuting him for insulting the religion of the Italian state — is an appropriate tribute to his genius. It pays proper attention to the influential position he held in an Italy whose special relationship with God was liable to falter whenever someone happened along with promises of *dolce vita*. Pasolini was seen as carrying just such a seductive message. To many on the Right he personified all that was devilish on the Left. The press adopted the adjective 'Pasolinian' to describe low-life and vice in general. The Italian Communist Party (not unlike our own Labour Party) found it could not endure the discomfort of having an openly gay spokesman for its values. To its lasting shame, it expelled Pasolini for his 'moral and political unworthiness'.

Pasolini associated heterosexuality with the middle class. In his rage against the bourgeoisification of Italian culture, he opposed the complacent 'permissiveness' of the Sixties, which sought to ape Anglo-American manners. He saw the so-called sexual revolution as a means to the heterosexualisation of Italian boys. As long as young women were in purdah, boys were on the loose; boys are available when girls are not. So Pasolini seems to have thought it was in his interests to oppose women's influence over their own sexual well-being. Abortion and contraception facilitate heterosexuality and erode the traditional Italian tolerance of homosexual intercourse between male teenagers. Gay sex should be the Italian man's principal method of contraception.

Long before it was possible to take for granted the interrelation of language, sexuality and politics (that Holiest of Trinities or degenerate *ménage à trois*, depending on your point of view), Pasolini was forging a version of Italian speech that became literally scandalous. Dogged by the press throughout the years of his fame, he provided a seemingly incessant source of fodder for the columnists, muck for the rakes. The variety of his talent — in Italy he is as well known for his poetry, fiction and drama as for his films — is matched by the capricious and contradictory response of his audience. Expelled by the Communists, he made a film approved of by the Vatican Curia; condemned for blasphemy by the Church, he was lionised by leftist intellectuals; loved by the street boys, he died at their hands.

This is not an English liberal biography (like, say, P.N. Furbank on E.M. Forster), full of comforting period detail and fragments of redundant *bon mot*. Siciliano is not an objective stranger: he plays a discreet bit-part in the account. (From a participant, I would have hoped for a far more gossipy account than this; academic biography can be left to the detached cultural historians who never knew the corpse.) More importantly, he takes firm control of his material and, more or less in accordance with the tendency of his subject, imposes a strictly Oedipal psychoanalytic line on it. To doubt this line is to suspect the failure of the whole enterprise.

Where I most angrily part company from Siciliano is in his treatment of Pasolini's murder. The biography starts and ends with it, thereby allowing a perverse *post hoc propter hoc* reasoning to colour the rest of the book: Pasolini's life was, as it were, doomed by the manner of his death. (A similar thing happens in Lahr's biography of Joe Orton, and in Katz's of Rainer Werner Fassbinder.) The suggestion that Pasolini — kicked in the balls, brained with a fence post and then driven over with his own car — committed 'suicide by proxy' (a suggestion at which the whole psychological thrust of this book is aimed) seems to me a monstrously offensive justification for deadly queer-bashing. Alberto Moravia's alternative theory, that this was the *murderer's* roundabout way of committing suicide, is slightly more ingenious, but crap all the same.

Do not look here for a leftist enquiry into why subproletarian males of a certain age need to kill gay men. Siciliano's last sentence is an extraordinary monument to homophobia, not only in its violent physical expression but also in its complacent intellectual form: 'Perhaps his death was his courageous way of asking the world to "know" him, even when it no longer "wanted" him.'

ANGEL OF PUBERTY

Umberto Saba, *Ernesto* (Manchester: Carcanet, 1987)

When choosing a title for their 1982 anthology of Italian gay
poetry, Renzo Paris and Antonio Veneziani settled on the phrase
L'amicizia amorosa, loving friendship, a quotation from a poem
by Umberto Saba (1883-1957). Saba was not the gayest writer
in the world — a large part of his fame rests on poems he wrote
about and for his wife Lina — but he was quite gay enough to
be palatable. In fact, he was the kind of bisexual man who enters
into a happy and lasting marriage with one woman, but whose
eye, when it roves, tends to be attracted to the adolescent male.
Lina notwithstanding, Saba was one of this century's outstanding
connoisseurs of the teenaged boy.

His great collection of poems *Il canzoniere* has a kind of
Angel of Puberty swooping and swooning over it: a cupid with
ruffled feathers, scuffed shoes, and the sort of lips which can't
sulk for long without breaking into a heart-stopping grin. Boys
appear in lovesick ones or loving twos; whole gangs of them kiss
each other when goals are scored. (None of this gets into
Carcanet's rather dull selection, *Thirty-one Poems*.)

Saba's verse tends to be autobiographical. The boys who are
loved in his poems are the boys he loved. Ordered chronologically,
they grace his life from the time of his own puberty (as in 'Un
ricordo', a poem which recalls a boyhood friendship he now
recognises as his first love affair) to old age (as in 'Un vecchio
amava un ragazzo': an old man loved a boy).

Late in life, after he had virtually given up writing poetry,
Saba began the short novel *Ernesto*, which revisits the scenes
and moods of his puberty. It is either strictly autobiographical
or an extreme example of retrospective wish-fulfilment.
Chronicling the main character's sexual growth, it constitutes
yet another proof of the basic continuity in Mediterranean sexual
habits since ancient Greece — a continuity which is only now
being broken by, among other influences, the Gay Movement.
The sequence is, in its way, as codified as any straight courtship.

Ernesto starts as passively homosexual, draping his virginity
over a flour sack to offer it to a man he works with. A barber
traumatises him by giving him — prematurely, in his own opinion
— his first shave, thereby catapulting him unwillingly into

adulthood. He therefore withdraws from the homosexual relationship and sets out to discover heterosex in the lap of a prostitute. Finally — as the incomplete manuscript peters out — he meets and starts to love a younger male friend; and we get a brief glimpse of a girl who will eventually become Ernesto's wife.

Set in Trieste, a city as divided and confused as the Danzig/ Gdansk of Günter Grass, the book associates adolescent awkwardness and enthusiasm with the youth of the Italian nation itself. Socialism is seen as the politics of boyhood, and its ideals are looked back on with nostalgia as something which can no more be recaptured than the vigour of one's teens, sexy but out of reach. Despite the urban setting, the book reads as a pastoral elegy, wistful, reactionary, with little patience for anything beyond its own lambent eroticism, which seems to have been born out of Longus by way of Sigmund Freud.

Translated and meticulously edited by Mark Thompson, with notes, a bibliography and a selection of Saba's letters, this edition suffers only from being in English — which obviously can't be helped. We know how the exquisite profanities of Jean Genet, when translated into English, often sound like the fake cockney speech one gets in *My Fair Lady*. Thompson has avoided this trap by virtually ignoring Saba's use of Triestese dialect. This stratagem dulls the dialogue, especially the awkward little conversations which are foreplay to the early scenes of buggery, but at least it avoids outright howlers.

Saba is no novelist. *Ernesto* is technically primitive. But as a humane defence of the powers of love it is impeccable; and it leads one back to *Il canzoniere* with renewed enthusiasm. Another substantial gay classic for the lists.

TRUE LOVE

Paul Monette, *Borrowed Time* (London: Collins Harvill, 1988)

In March 1985, after a period of intermittent ill-health, Roger Horwitz was diagnosed as having AIDS. He died in October 1986. *Borrowed Time* is his lover's memoir of the calamity they shared. The story involves a gruelling physical descent from weakness and weight loss, via initial tests and rumours, through recurrent lung infection (PCP), blindness, incontinence, the threat of dementia, to death itself.

Their emotional struggle involves coping not only with illness itself, but also with myth, the insensitivity of medics, the deaths of friends, the need to keep the disease secret at a time of media panic, thoughts of suicide, and so on. With the experience of coming out as homosexual behind them, they now find they have to come out again, first to themselves and then to others, as being HIV positive, and then as having developed AIDS. Monette is particularly sensitive to the feelings of Horwitz's parents: having once accepted only slowly the fact that he was gay, they now have to find the courage not to think of his sexuality as mere doom.

Monette is aware of his and his lover's relatively favoured situation. 'In this enterprise we were fortunate to have privileges: we knew the right people and had enough money.' Indeed, one of the book's consistent horrors is the extent to which they had to rely on such privilege. After barely surviving the toxicity of the drug Suramin, Horwitz became the first patient west of the Mississippi to be put on AZT, this as a consequence of rumours from the east, behind-scenes persuasion, and a healthy bank balance. Jockeying for drugs becomes a central part of the nightmare: since the US Government has turned drug research over to private industry, the nature of one's treatment is determined by the market. The grotesque result is seen in Monette's account of smuggling missions to buy drugs in Mexico.

The book is written in rather restless, obsessively metaphorical prose. This is obtrusive at first, but the subject soon muscles in with its own momentum. Since both men kept diaries, the account is detailed; and Monette has dutifully checked his own impressions against the memories of relatives and friends. This was his way of negotiating grief and the continuing threat to his own health. Other projects helped, too. During the final weeks of Horwitz's life, Monette anchored himself to 'normality' by writing the novelization of an Arnold Schwarzenegger movie.

To write about AIDS is largely a question of bearing witness. (This clearly evokes a parallel with Holocaust memoirs.) As Monette says, 'We cannot all go down to defeat and darkness, we have to say we have been here.' The fact that gay men have a voice with which to do so is one of the great triumphs of the Gay Movement in the western democracies. The Seventies gave us, not our vulnerability to AIDS, but the strength to fight it. This is where one must locate the real threat of gagging measures like Clause 28: for we have learnt from our own history that (as the current slogan has it) Silence = Death.

Monette has served Roger Horwitz as well after death as he did before. (He has also published a collection of elegies to his memory.) Homophobes who do not want their minds changed had better steer clear: *Borrowed Time* is a massive affirmation of true love. It is also an incitement to action. As Monette says, in referring to the courage of Winnie Mandela: 'They take your life away whether you fight or not, so you might as well fight.' A less robust survivor, succumbing to despair, could have said you might as well *not*.

BRILLIANT AND CORROSIVE

Neil Bartlett, *Who Was That Man? A Present for Mr Oscar Wilde*
(London: Serpent's Tail, 1988)
Jonathan Goodman (ed), *The Oscar Wilde File* (London: Allison
and Busby, 1988)
Vyvyan Holland, *Oscar Wilde* (London: Thames and Hudson,
1988)
Oscar Wilde, *The Ballad of Reading Gaol* (London: Journeyman,
1978)
Oscar Wilde, *The Soul of Man Under Socialism* (London:
Journeyman, 1988)

The debate on whether a writer's homosexuality 'matters' must,
I suppose, be won or lost on the case of Oscar Wilde. As the
definitive 'unspeakable of the Oscar Wilde sort' (to quote Forster's
Maurice), he occupies a unique place in this country's sexual and
literary history. His name crops up in the adolescent passages
of countless biographies. In 1915, the 18 year-old Michael
Davidson imagined only he and Wilde had been born homosexual.
A little later, John Betjeman was warned by his mother about
'a man called Oscar Wilde'. (The name alone was sufficient
substitute for that of the love that dared not speak its own.) Even
in Friuli in the late 1930s, the liceo student Pier Paolo Pasolini,
already acquainted at first hand with other boys' bodies, first
learnt of the social disadvantage of being homosexual when a
friend told him about Wilde's trial.

    In short, Wilde is the best-known homosexual of all. He is
also one of an increasing number of writers around whom an
industry is maintained without there being evidence of
widespread interest in their written work. Since the scandal of
his trial and imprisonment is, therefore, crucial to his status in
modern memory, it is hard to imagine a useful book about him
ignoring his homosexuality.

    But, amazingly, this central fact goes unacknowledged in
Vyvyan Holland's re-telling of the famous life history. His book
(a reprint of the 1960 *Oscar Wilde and His World*) makes no
real sense of the events of 1895, and obviously assumes that
Wilde's work can be read and understood without any such
contextual back-up. This sleight of hand results in the kind of
text that certain recent legislators would doubtless recommend

for our schools: a censorious travesty. Of course, Holland, as
Wilde's son, was in a peculiar position *vis-à-vis* the writer's moral
reputation; so his problem is, to that extent, excusable.

The Oscar Wilde File, by way of contrast, is wholly reliant
on the trials. A rather purposeless compilation of contemporary
newspaper reports, it comes from the Let's-Throw-a-Book-
Together school of English letters. Since Jonathan Goodman is
a 'crime historian', it is being marketed as some kind of real life
whodunnit, in a field where only a detailed *what-was-it-he-dun*
would be at all new. The reports themselves, hamstrung by
Victorian propriety, yield far less than we have since discovered
from fuller transcriptions of the case.

It is left to two really magisterial *Daily Telegraph* editorials
(6 April and 27 May 1895) on the nature of modern art to liven
things up. The sharpness of their attack on Wilde's use of 'brilliant
paradoxes and corrosive epigrams' renews one's faith in the
dangerousness of mere figures of speech. The writer clearly
believed that what Wilde did with his words was as 'filthy' as
what he did with young men's bodies. The latter merely served
to prove the former.

A Wildean degree of *chutzpah* may have passed by
heterosexual means to Vyvyan Holland; but it seems to have
descended in even greater measure, 'homosexually', to Neil
Bartlett. *Who Was That Man?* starts from the point Holland left
out: that Wilde 'is famous above all else for being a homosexual'.
To this premise he adds a second, that he, too, is homosexual,
and that he can therefore speak of 'that part of my history which
is called "Oscar Wilde" '.

What follows is part biography, part autobiography, part
gay guide to the metropolis. Some readers will choose to be put
off by the fact that Bartlett is addressing his fellow gay men,
present and past, as 'we'. In doing so, he attests not only to
Wilde's desires and their social context, but also to a vibrant
continuity of homosexual history. The way he overlays the map
of our own disco-studded London on the restaurants and molly-
houses of Wilde's is consistently moving. One begins to see the
reality of Wilde's 'hidden' life at last. Even if the green carnation
is not an exact equivalent of the Marlboro packet, one can
appreciate the tenuous line of resemblance between the two.

Bartlett is also hypothetical in ways which, if not
academically rigorous, open rich seams of speculative thought.
A good example is when he asks, 'What would our culture as

gay men in this city have been like if Wilde had still been living
and writing in London in the 1920s, if his career as a homosexual
artist had been as long as, say, André Gide's?' It is not a point
he follows up in any detail; but it has already served its purpose.
It is, simply, a good question.

Bartlett's best quality is his humaneness. The weight of
sympathy with which he describes, say, the Boulton and Park
scandal makes it sound, for a change, as if real people were
involved. So, although the book is capricious and incomplete,
alternately touching and exasperating, it makes an elegant and
intelligent shelf-mate to the Richard Ellmann biography.
Whether or not you appreciate it may give a good indication of
how you would really have felt about Wilde himself.

The net effect should be that one goes back to Wilde's texts
with a heightened sensitivity to the personal dimension behind
their gloss. And, indeed, *The Ballad of Reading Gaol* now seems
a little like one of the prison poems of Jean Genet, whittled down
to the sentimental core. Similarly, *The Soul of Man Under
Socialism*, post-Bartlett, is enriched by what its poise tries to
conceal. As a political essay, it is easily slick enough to grace a
politician's autocue, where the world's complexity resolves itself
down to platitude. But look at the subjects Wilde touches on: the
punishment of crime, the redundancy of matrimony, the intrusive
powers of the press ('In old days men had the rack. Now they
have the press.') and so on. Behind the glibness, there is a note
of anticipatory panic.

THE AIDS UNIVERSE

Robert Ferro, *Second Son* (London: Hutchinson, 1988)

Mark learns he has AIDS; he meets Bill, who is in the same situation; they fall in love. Adding breadth to this basic story-line are, on the one hand, the reactions of Mark's family to his illness, and on the other, Bill's mellowing grief for the recent death of his lover Fred.

Such is the substance of the late Robert Ferro's last novel. It leads straight into all sorts of important issues about what the literature of AIDS is supposed to be doing, and what it can legitimately be expected to do. I have heard all the lies about AIDS, and now I want to know the truth. But is a work of fiction ever true enough? This question and the doubt it implies loom over my reading of *Second Son* much as they loom over fiction about Nazi genocide.

As in Adam Mars-Jones and Edmund White's *The Darker Proof*, the syndrome is not named. This is a policy I do not really understand, unless it is designed to remove fiction about AIDS from the particular historical and social circumstances that connived to give it its name — in other words to 'universalise' the crisis; in effect, to render it uncritical.

But we all know that AIDS is menacing in two main respects: firstly in its physical effect on the individual, and secondly in its social existence. To deprive it of the latter is to falsify a whole set of circumstances in which people with HIV or ARC or AIDS (distinctions which presumably can't be made in the universe of the nameless disease) find themselves having to live.

AIDS literature surely ought to take cognisance of the babble of names with which the crisis has developed, from vague notions of a 'gay cancer', to GRID, to AIDS, to the 'gay plague' and beyond, and from HTLV3 to HIV. AIDS becomes SIDA; A-*zee*-T becomes A-*zed*-T. Elsewhere, you have to speak of 'Slim'. The names spell out the history (and geography) of our knowledge of what is going on. The names delineate the specific social circumstances of time and place. Besides which, if we refuse to name it, isn't there a danger of AIDS becoming the disease that dare not speak its name?

Anyway, why 'universalise'? Is that not on a par with making AIDS available to the 'general public': making it palatable to white straights, selling more copies? The trouble with the universalising tendency — as others have said before me — is that, at worst, it is pandering to the requirement of WASP men that minorities deprive themselves of the right to a distinctive voice; at best, it becomes generalised and apolitical.

Now, a fictional character is an extended metaphor for a hypothetical real person. All metaphorical writing consists of both tenor and vehicle: both the metaphor and the reality behind it, which it is seeking to express. But gay writers know, perhaps better than most, that metaphor can be used to conceal as well as reveal. And this is where the problem arises in imaginative literature which is dealing with sensitive areas of reality: does its fictive nature, its artistry, help us to see the real situation more clearly than a documentary would, or does it merely decorate, and thereby obscure, the truth, like plaster foliage around a load-bearing beam?

Perhaps — in much the same way as it makes a vital difference if Holocaust literature was written by an actual survivor of the *univers concentrationnaire* — we need to know that *Second Son* was written by a PWA. Perhaps Ferro's illness is, then, the necessary ghost at this particular banquet.

Of course, there is an inevitable *frisson* of sadness about the act of reading such a book, after its author's death, a book dedicated to the lover who died first, about two men living with the disease with which the author and his lover were both living when the book was written and published and promoted. To read it sympathetically — as an urban gay man at some risk, and with friends and lovers at similar or greater risk, of the same fate — is to allow the book to do its worst — or best — with one's body, from tear ducts to guts. Afterwards, one may resent the temporary power it managed to exert. But how much of this has to do with the aesthetics of the case?

I do not think we need to patronise Ferro's memory by pretending *Second Son* is better than it really is. The fact is that the circumstances of its writing are even more impressive than the book itself; or rather, the circumstances form a large part of what makes the book impressive. After all, in spite of the intrusion of AIDS, *Second Son* is to some extent a rewrite of major elements of *The Blue Star* (1985) and that marvellous debut *The Family of Max Desir* (1983). Ferro's range was narrow. (He could never, for instance, write about people without money.) So readers who know his previous books will recognise many characteristics: his strong sense of place, usually sited in a seaside house; his irritating tendency to use his Italian origins as a kind of cultural chic; his very Italianate veneration of the extended family; the theme of the dead or dying mother; landscape gardening . . .

At some point, I suppose, we may have to accept that any writing by those most closely involved in AIDS can never — *must* never — be entirely polished. The author's eye needs to be firmly fixed on the chaos and hurt of the now, rather than on the rigorous aesthetic demands of some irrelevant posterity. Attend to the living and the dying: good literature will survive of its own accord. Paul Monette's book of elegies on his lover Roger Horwitz, *Love Alone* (1988), is better than his earlier collections of verse precisely *because* it is so raw, angry, uncorrected. One of the problems with *Second Son* is that, in a situation which seems to be calling for jagged rage, Ferro was still trying to polish and refine. But at least this means that where he fails he does so by his own unfailingly high standards.

When he is not burdening his narrative with unnecessary literary effects which occasionally blow up in his face (I have still not been able to make any sense at all of the first sentence in Part Two) Ferro handles his themes with extraordinary finesse. I cannot imagine such painful sensitivity being achieved by any gay British author writing today. In this respect Ferro and one or two other contemporary Americans are more truly the beneficiaries of Bloomsbury (of Forster and Woolf in particular) than anyone in Britain.

At the book's emotional heart is a stay in a cabin on a lake, where Bill and Mark scatter Fred's ashes. Ferro is completely the master of this sequence. He liked to think of himself as a 'fabulist', and it is true that these pages are fabulous in any sense. Characteristically, the author is conscious of literary precedent: the text that hangs behind these scenes is Henry David Thoreau's *Walden* (1854), where all the mythic possibilities of life on the American continent were lived out by one man on the fringes of a lake in Massachusetts.

Towards the end of that book, Thoreau wrote: 'If a man does not keep pace with his companions, perhaps it is because he hears a different drummer. Let him step to the music which he hears, however measured or far away'. For better or worse, Ferro kept pace with his own drum in a manner which gave him, in the books he left, a distinct voice and a searching sensibility which had barely begun to establish their deserved place in our literature. We are left with tantalising traces of the really good writer he might have become.

JAMES BALDWIN 1924-1987

Remembering Baldwin, it makes sense not to overlook the notorious attack on him launched by Eldridge Cleaver in *Soul on Ice* (1968). Cleaver found in Baldwin's work 'the most gruelling, agonizing, total hatred of the blacks, particularly of himself, and the most shameful, fanatical, fawning, sycophantic love of the whites that one can find in the writings of any black American writer of note in our time'.

As we read on, it does not take long to see that Cleaver's objection is as much sexual as racial: he cannot cope with the idea of a black man who is gay. Such men, he says, suffer from a 'racial death-wish'. Many of them are 'outraged and frustrated because in their sickness they are unable to have a baby by a white man'. As if we have not yet understood his attitude, he adds that 'Homosexuality is a sickness, just as are baby-rape or wanting to become the head of General Motors'.

The real sin, according to the Cleaver hatchet-job, is not so much homosexuality — though that is bad enough — as homosexual miscegenation with the white man on top. (Cleaver's pride in his own phallic power involved the most profound contempt for anyone penises entered.) While Baldwin would argue, as he did in 1972, that 'people do not fall in love according to their color', Cleaver might have replied that they should.

It is true that Baldwin's fiction, on a superficial reading, often seemed suspiciously easy for white readers to stomach. But the liberal reading of his books was never particularly plausible. He was not saying what white liberals liked to think he was : something vaguely to the effect of 'Here we all are, white and black, gay and straight, all essentially the same as one another, and when we have put aside our differences, all we'll need is love'. That kind of message has only ever looked substantial in the limited measure of song lyrics.

Baldwin was far too frustrated and angry to mean anything so trivial. He saw American racism as having tangled sexual roots. As he says in *No Name in the Street* (1972), 'white men, who invented the nigger's big black prick, are still at the mercy of this nightmare, and are still, for the most part, doomed, in one way or another, to attempt to make this prick their own'. The way to do this was to keep power out of the hands of black men: to keep them impotent. Hence that favourite accompaniment to racist lynchings in the Southern states: castration.

Baldwin's attitude to the United States was both engaged and enraged. As he says in one of his poems, the dignified symbols of state have a very different meaning to people the state oppresses:

> I've SEEN some stars.
> I've GOT some stripes.

He moved to Europe because he was tired of being defined according to other people's categorical values. As he explained in 1959, 'I left America because I doubted my ability to survive the fury of the color problem. I wanted to prevent myself from becoming merely a Negro; or, even, merely a Negro writer. I wanted to find out in what way the *specialness* of my experience could be made to connect me with other people instead of dividing me from them'.

This concern with avoiding the easy labelling of people goes to the heart of what he was trying to do in his fiction. As long ago as 1949, Baldwin published in Morocco an essay on homosexuality and fiction in America (inexcusably not reprinted in his collected essays, *The Price of the Ticket*) which anticipates many of the arguments of the Women's and Gay movements in the sixties and seventies. The problem is not, he says, homosexuality itself, but the disordered relations between heterosexual women and men, which lead ultimately to a 'panic close to madness' we now sometimes call homophobia. The problem is not the homosexual man, but the heterosexual American tough guy's irrational and violent *fear* of homosexual men.

Baldwin then lashes out at the macho ethos of the fiction of people like James M. Cain and Raymond Chandler, which can only lead to a sexual brutality of which women and homosexual men are the victims. His conclusions are simple: 'It is quite impossible to write a worthwhile novel about a Jew or a Gentile or a Homosexual' (or, we are expected to add, a black person) 'for people refuse, unhappily, to function in so neat and one-dimensional a fashion'. 'A novel insistently demands the presence and passion of human beings, who cannot ever be labeled'.

So, contrary to the critics of that time, Baldwin's novel *Giovanni's Room* (1956) was not intended as a novel about The

Homosexual, even if it was about (white) gay men. This and
Another Country (1962) were the two novels which most offended
the labellers' sense of purity. The latter is about a chain of affairs
and betrayals involving black and white, gay and straight, women
and men. (It would make a stupendous opera.) Both of these
books are written against the kind of categorisations favoured
by more orderly (and ordinary) political minds than Baldwin's.
Like so many who became active in the Civil Rights movement,
he always resisted the logic of those who wanted, for the sake of
political purity — and, let's face it, *racial* purity — to replace
segregation with separatism.

Another characteristic of Baldwin's which has tended to hold
back his literary and political reputations is his emotionalism.
'Brilliance without passion,' he said, 'is nothing more than
sterility'. But his rages have always upset his literary critics, and
his sentimentality his political critics. The Man of Feeling is in
an unhappy position in modern culture: for any feeling displayed
is seen as being either infantile or insincere.

The two Americas, black and white, never really forgave
Baldwin his third dimension. Those who wanted him to be a
conventional black American writer, to whom they could respond
with formulaic ease, found instead a laughing and weeping
Frenchified faggot, as critical of black homophobia and
antisemitism as he was of white supremacy. It was the freedoms
he demanded for himself — to live and love and write as he
chose, thereby violating not only the proprieties of the hegemony
but also those of its subverters — that ultimately limited his
reputation.

THE PURSUIT OF SIGNIFICANCE

Michel Tournier, *The Golden Droplet* (London: Methuen, 1988)

This novel is about an Arab boy called Idris. From the moment when a blonde woman tourist in tiny shorts takes a photograph of him and drives off across the desert, Idris embarks on a quest: for the future's objects of desire, the woman and (his image of) himself. From the moment when his friend Ibrahim, naked, covered in camel gore and joyously sporting a hard-on, gets swallowed by sand and buried alive, Idris embarks on a pilgrimage: for the past's bloody sources of desire, the womb and the rectum, blood and guts.

The narrative follows the youth northwards from his oasis, via Oran and Marseille (where he loses his virginity and his golden droplet to a female whore), to Paris, imperial capital of the Empire of Signs. Here, Idris finds his image is in constant demand — from a gay film director, from a shop display manager in search of new dummies, and from a fetishist who collects, photographs and loves boy-dummies. Idris is immortalised on celluloid and immersed in liquid plastic to be mass-produced. He is victimised by people who value their images of him more than they value him; him they hardly see.

Tournier shows how the ancient belief, that to steal someone's image is to steal their soul, is no 'primitive superstition' but an increasingly serious problem in the age of television and advertising. If he were a lesser writer you might swear he had just read Roland Barthes and Susan Sontag on photography. (Actually, he has written two books on the art himself.) But he is one of the best novelists working in France today. He has lived at the centre of a great academic and cultural whirlwind, friend to the likes of Foucault and Deleuze — though he claims to read their work more out of friendship than out of interest.

The main raw materials of his work tend to be not situations or characters so much as ideas. He is a novelist with a semiologist's imagination. Umberto Eco is an intellectual who writes novels; Tournier is an intellectual novelist. He was being less than honest when, asked if he was interested in structuralism, he replied 'Yes, a little'; and asked if he was interested in psychoanalysis, he replied 'Yes, even less'. Such things intrigue him, whether or not he cares to admit it.

Tournier is relentless in the pursuit of significance; there are times when one wishes he would relax and allow something meaningless to occur. His mytholatry is occasionally tiresome when it gets in the way of our view of his characters. But for the most part he manages to entwine myth and 'real life' with a lightness of touch that, at its very best, reminds me of the Arabian Nights. At least all the myths he concerns himself with are living: those of the antique world do not interest him, except where they encroach on the present day.

French gay writers have a long tradition of fascination with Arab culture, at least insofar as it shapes the lives and limbs of Arab boys. As representative examples, we need only recall André Gide's *The Immoralist* (1902) or the late Guy Hocquenghem's *Love in Relief* (1982). Although more ambitious than Tournier's book, and more dramatically plotted, the latter is another account of an Arab youth at large in the Western world of images and signs. But Hocquenghem's central character has to read the Western world through any but the sense for which it was all designed: he is blind. This puts him at a disadvantage in relation to other people, of course, but also at an advantage: for he is not so readily entranced by visual spells.

One reason for Tournier's interest in the Third World is that it proves his belief that there is, or should be, no such thing as homosexuality. In the Arab communities, for instance, 'il n'y a pas d'homosexualité parce qu'il n'y a pas d'heterosexualité'. Thus, he finds the subject of homosexuality less interesting in itself than as a window which gives a view onto heterosexuality. The latter can only exist in the august presence of the former.

This results in another typically French characteristic: the resistance to any hint of a gay ghetto. Yves Navarre once said 'I am a writer. I am gay. I am not a gay writer.' Tournier, too, would be distressed to be pigeon-holed as a gay writer. Well, I can only counter that it is not the writer but the reader who decides these things.

Just look at Tournier's novels. *Friday* is a post-Freudian version of *Robinson Crusoe* in which the whole island is eroticised in relation to its castaway's virility. (How far is he still heterosexual when fucking a landscape on which he imposes an imaginary female gender? Or when he becomes jealous of the island itself because his beloved Friday has started following his sexual example?) *The Erl King* is about a cloacally obsessive paedophile monster who bathes in boys' hair. *Gemini* concentrates on a pair of twins, one straight and one gay, in a way which is far more searching and profound than Bruce Chatwin manages in *On the Black Hill* (or, for that matter, Philip Ridley in *Crocodilia*); but the book is almost hijacked by Alexandre, a mad queen who makes a kingdom of the rubbish dump he lives on. (Tournier claims Alexandre is the only homosexual character he has created.) In *The Four Wise Men* one of the Magi endures 33 years in the salt-mines of Sodom.

And now, in *The Golden Droplet*, Tournier hovers around the image of a mainly heterosexual youth in a way which illuminates the whole matter of sexual identity. As in the case of his version of Crusoe, Tournier portrays a heterosexuality which is not set above or apart from homosexuality: the two exist in interconnected forms. Throughout his career, one of his most consistently interesting themes has been the *complicated* nature of identity and sexuality. If this results in complicated books, so much the better. We get enough simplification in the tabloids.

There is more gay fiction in these fictions than you would find in the work of many a popular gay novelist. Whether or not their author is homo- or bisexual is a matter between himself and his duvet cover. But you have to conclude that, even if not a gay novelist, Michel Tournier is a gay novelist all the same.

THE QUEER WITH THE BOW TIE

Ian Gibson, *Federico Garcia Lorca: A Life* (London: Faber, 1989)

I have seen the ghost of Lorca stalking through this book. He walks through walls, he rattles his chains, he sometimes even goes *boo*. But he is incorporeal: barely visible at all.

The book is a triumph, of course; a massive product of scholarly tenacity and love. It is inconceivable that any future work on Lorca could ignore it. To that extent, it is absolutely definitive. But it is a work of pure scholarship, and that is part of the problem. Gibson has been, I think, too much of the meticulous and conscientious researcher and not enough of the fabulist. Where his research draws a blank he is lost for words, so he moves on. Yet biography — the life of the dead — has, of necessity, to be an act not only of verification, but also of imagination.

Take the matter with which I am most concerned here, that of the poet's homosexuality. Lorca was as homosexual as he was Spanish. Try reading him as a *German* and you will see how ridiculous it would be to 'overlook' his sexual orientation. But even acknowledging it, Gibson is in trouble from the start. In his introduction he has to admit to having been stymied by the 'discretion' of relatives and friends. Some don't want to talk about Lorca's homosexuality; others don't even want to believe in it. The family of one of the poet's boyfriends went so far as to destroy not only inscribed copies of the poet's books, but even a manuscript poem.

In this respect, we cannot judge Gibson by standards of post-Stonewall openness. He has done his best — and his best is extraordinary — in the face of stubborn Iberian homophobia. (Don't be misled into thinking that all of Spain is taking part in a Pedro Almodovar film.) In spite of silences, he manages to name and describe Lorca's principal boyfriends and the other gay figures with whom he should culturally be associated.

Where Gibson fails — and this is not for want of trying — is in the portrayal of Lorca as a *homosexual personality*. For instance, he is late to get to the point. He writes that the poet 'was already acutely aware of his sexual peculiarity' at the age of 20. (What on earth is that 'already' meant to mean?) We do not see him eyeing up other men until he is 27, though the poetry shows ample evidence of a roving eye.

A lot of Gibson's most important phrases are suggestive but imprecise. He keeps mentioning the poet's 'anguish concerning his homosexuality' but does not delve into the nature of this anguish; it is as though the reader were expected to assume a link between homosexuality and anguish and merely to nod with sympathetic understanding. At the age of 27 Lorca was still trying to 'come to terms with his homosexuality'. Fine. It is, of course, a phrase we recognise; but it means different things in different cases. It means nothing on its own. I want to know what was stopping this 'coming to terms' and what shape the struggle took.

Several times, apparently, Lorca attempted to fuck Salvador Dali. By the painter's own account, 'That upset me a lot because I was not a pederast, and had no intention of giving in. It hurt, moreover. And so nothing happened. But I was very flattered from the point of view of my personal prestige.' In the context of their relationship as described by Gibson, this is unconvincing: it seems to me to raise a number of questions, all unasked, about how two intimate friends (one gay, the other trying not to teeter on the brink) could end up behaving like this. I do not believe Lorca was a rapist; what we need to know — to decide for ourselves, if the documents don't help — is what happened *before* Dali's rectitude put a padlock on his rectum? What made Lorca think the adventure was worth trying? Wine? Had they already made love in other ways? The psychological evidence and strategic likelihood suggest to me that they had.

Lorca worked for a long time on a play called *The Destruction of Sodom* by comparison with which he thought Oscar Wilde would seem 'an out of date, fat and pusillanimous old queen'. This is, I think, the only hint in the whole book (and it is not a clue Gibson seems to notice) that Lorca, in attacking royalty, spoke the language of queens. This brings me to the biography's main lapse, which it shares with Paul Binding's *Lorca: The Gay Imagination* (GMP, 1986). Gibson does not see any need to introduce the concept of Camp. (He uses the word only once, Binding only twice.) This seriously limits his chances of being able to characterise the tone of Lorca's voice in much of his verse; not to mention, I would guess, his conversation. In a 1980 interview in *Gay Sunshine*, Jaime Gil de Biedma said, 'Lorca loathed screaming queens, and that's what he himself was'. Indeed, Lorca's self-loathing can equal Genet's in its ornateness.

I do not mean to give the impression of an anguished Lorca, morose with self-disgust. Pablo Neruda said nobody loved laughter more. This is omitted from both Binding's and Gibson's accounts: the conscious hilarity of his High Camp seriousness. I find it hard to accept Binding's use of Henry James's phrase 'the figure in the carpet' to describe the relation of the poet's sexuality to the less explicit works. As in Cocteau, the mannered stratagems of Camp make homosexuality not just the figure, but every thread in the carpet and every plank in the floor beneath.

However, I don't want to sound entirely negative about Gibson's version of Lorca's 'private' life. He does liven things up a bit when making personal readings of some of Dali's paintings, and is rather good on the hypocrisy of Lorca's anti-gay gay poem the 'Ode to Walt Whitman' (of which Whitman would not have approved). Also useful are his revelations about the homophobic Luis Bunuel, who spent part of his youth queer-bashing in Madrid, and who described Lorca's poetry as 'the kind of thing that keeps Spanish beds full of menstrual blood'.

But if you want to read a great biography on a great gay poet you will have to ask many of the more searching, human questions for yourself. Read between the lines, with the poems open at one side and your imagination open at the other. There is still a lot more to be said about this man who, in the months before his assassination, was known to elements of the Granadan bourgeoisie as 'The Queer with the Bow Tie'; and who, on the evidence of station signs, thought every town in England was called Bovril. Here are the facts of the life; now they need life breathing into them.

PRISONERS OF CONSCIENCE

Cherrill Hicks, *Who Cares: Looking After People at Home* (London: Virago, 1989)

Let me start, as Hicks does, with the spectacular statistics. There are now 1.3 million full-time 'carers' in Britain, and between five and six million more for whom caring is a major responsibility. (Of these, only 81,000 receive Invalid Care Allowance.) In most families, one person takes on this role, unhelped by the others.

Most of these individuals are middle-aged or old, and most are women. Seventy percent of them suffer physical injury, mostly to their backs, while caring. Four out of five receive no help at all. Two thirds of them are in generally poor health, and half are in danger of becoming mentally ill. About 10,000 young people under eighteen have major responsibility for caring for a disabled parent.

All these people, generally quiet to the point of invisibility, save the state £11 billion a year. And their numbers are bound to increase. There has been a 500 percent increase in old people since 1900. Advances in medical science have ensured that the 'handicapped' live longer than they used to. Government policy is increasingly geared towards returning those who need looking after to the 'community'.

Using material gathered from over eighty interviews with carers, as well as from previous surveys, Hicks takes a systematic look at the main types of carer: married women looking after old relatives, most often theior parents or parents-in-law; women looking after disabled husbands; parents with disabled children; old parents caring for their adult offspring; male carers; carers in the ethnic minorities.

On men, Hicks speaks of caring husbands and sons, and gay men looking after lovers with AIDS. On black and Asian carers, she concentrates on the different attitudes to age and illness in Britain from those which prevail in her subjects' countries of origin; and on young women brought to Britain in arranged marriages, now having to look after in-laws without support or even contact from their own families.

The book also deals with funding and other (invariably inadequate) matters of public policy. Hicks shows that the amount of support carers are given falls well short of even the meanest ideal. Even where support is available, typically, information about it is not.

Many married women are locked into a life-long cycle of having to care. Having brought up their children, they then have to cope with the old age of their own and their husbands' parents, after which they often end up nursing their own husbands. Others find their lives taken over by a single object of care: one of the women mentioned here gave up work at the age of 14 in order to look after her sick mother; she was still doing so at 75, when the mother was 99.

Much of what Hicks has to say goes wider than the issue of caring. It all underlines the appalling gender imbalance that prevails in our society. According to one survey, among married couples with a person to care for, wives spent three hours a day caring, while their husbands spent only 13 minutes doing so. Another telling statistic is that for couples in which the wife is caring for a disabled husband, divorce rates are lower than average; but where the husband is caring for a disabled wife, the rate is higher than average.

The book is also full of terrible stories about the failures of the health service and its labyrinthine bureaucracy. One sticks in my memory: 'One woman I knew didn't like to admit her husband took her to the toilet, so she told the doctor she crawled on her hands and knees. Because she said she could crawl to the loo, she was judged as being fit, and able to carry out bodily functions'.

You may have noticed that I've been using the adjective 'old'. Hicks often comments on the low esteem in which old people tend to be held in this country, and she contrasts the widespread disrespect and neglect with what happens in other cultures. But she keeps using the fearful euphemisms 'elderly' and 'aged' throughout the book, reinforcing the impression she is trying to undermine, that oldness is something to be ashamed of. It is high time old people dared to speak their name with at least as much confidence as our junior citizens do.

My other main complaint is that the section on AIDS seems to have crept in as an afterthought, and is informed by only one interview. If you have read other books on AIDS, fiction or non-fiction, or indeed if you have been personally involved in the epidemic, you will learn nothing from this part of Hicks's book. It is presumably aimed at people who have never yet thought about the subject.

Oddly, Hicks does not mention — contrary to the rest of the book's tendency to highlight the amount of caring that falls to women — that many people with AIDS are not gay men; nor is an increasing proportion of those who have to care for them. There is no mention of AIDS in the ethnic minorities chapter; nor, for that matter, of sickle cell anaemia.

However, the book as a whole does its job clearly and efficiently: it engages and informs, moves and sickens. It ends with a useful list of books and addresses. One of the interviewees, a daughter caring for her old mother, calls herself a prisoner of conscience. All the evidence shows that other carers are the same: trapped, often in loneliness and poverty, by their own moral virtue. Perhaps Amnesty International could ask the government the crucial question. Who cares for the carers?

PUERILE POETRY

John Gambril Nicholson, *In the Dreamy Afternoon* (London: GMP, 1989)

Paul Webb ends his introduction to this slim selection of poems as follows: 'Although Nicholson is an important representative of the gay poets of the 1890's, it is the timelessness of his experience of love, desire and rejection, and his skill in expressing this in verse, that has survived the passing of nearly one century, and will ensure that he is read and enjoyed by generations to come.' In a similar vein, the oddly dyslexic back-cover blurb ends: 'This collection transcends the boundaries of its confinement in history to express with beautiful and often highly comic lyricism the timelessness of love, desire and ultimate rejection.'

I don't believe either of these statements for a moment. I think they are a misguided way of promoting gay literature specific to one of the periods most crucial to the development of modern British gay culture: the decades immediately following the passing of the Labouchère Amendment, which criminalised gay sex. Furthermore, these statements manage both to overrate and to patronise Nicholson, who was by no stretch of the imagination a creator of what traditional critics mean when they speak of 'lasting' or 'eternal' works of art.

So, while I am delighted that GMP are bringing such poets back into print, the fact is that, like most of the Uranians, Nicholson stands or falls as a voice in history. There is nothing 'timeless' about his work at all. But if we value our history — as I try to, not always with equal conviction — we must value him and men like him. If not, we can dismiss him as a wretched versifier; in which case, he is not worth republishing.

It follows from the above that I think Paul Webb ought to have included in his introduction as much information on the poet as he could find, instead of the rather vague evaluative coments he seems to prefer. In his edition of E.E. Bradford's *To Boys Unknown* (GMP, 1988), Webb did at least provide a biographical and bibliographical note, albeit brief. But he seems to want to see both poets as not only 'outrageously camp' (one of the most overused and misused expressions in our culture), but camp from a 1980s' perspective only — as if the poets themselves were too naive to see how 'highly comic' (ridiculous?) their work really was.

Naivety is not a stable condition, any more than cunning is. Its artlessness is often disturbed by artful moments. I believe Frederick Rolfe recognised this in Nicholson's verse when he spoke of being flabbergasted by its 'blatant *naïveté'*. Blatancy implies awareness. There are times when Nicholson's awareness of boys' waywardness seems cynical. In such moments he knows exactly what he is doing.

Rolfe was a teacher at Saffron Walden Grammar School when Nicholson was a pupil there. They are said to have developed an 'intimate' relationship, which eventually cooled into friendship and, ultimately, into enmity. Nicholson himself earned his living as a schoolmaster. Like many of his contemporaries, he was a keen amateur photographer of boys.

He seems to have met many of the gay cultural figures of his time (J.A. Symonds at Henry Scott Tuke's house, for instance). And, while he always published his books in his own name, even if none of them had survived he would still appear in footnotes as one of the contributors (along with Oscar Wilde and Bosie Douglas) to the notorious single issue of the *Chameleon* which cropped up with such devastating effect when Wilde was on trial.

Such details — to which I don't have privileged access: they appear in Timothy d'Arch Smith's *Love in Earnest* — make up the context to Nicholson's text. Without it, he is nobody. Despite its subject, his poetry is utterly conventional; the only thing that commends it to our attention is that it is written to boys. Had these love poems been addressed to young women, I doubt that the most dedicated collector would pay them any attention. Their value is entirely dependent on social context.

As in so much of the literature of boy-love, the whole world participates in the author's desire. (I suppose Nicholson learned this mannerism from Theocritus and Vergil.) His boys inhabit landscapes which are themselves puerile, lavishly sown with sweet-william and ladslove, and heavy with the scent of mignonette and musk. The seasons correspond with the phases of boyhood. Buds open, stems thicken, plums ripen and start to ooze. At the sight of his crops' blond pubescence, a farmer's thoughts turn to harvest...

Nicholson's favourite adjective seems to be 'little'. He is charmed and turned on by the compactness of boyish flesh. (So the cover illustration of this edition seems inappropriately hairy and muscular.) But it is not only his boys' bodies that are little.

He seems to have loved the charm of nubile little minds, ripe to be inseminated with learning.

Hence his limited ambitions as a poet. The end of Nicholson's career is blithely indifferent to Modernism. To me, this is its saving grace. For one thing is perfectly clear about these poems, and it is this alone that makes them at all touching: the best of them are meant to be understood by the boys they address. One poem begins as follows:

> The world can never be empty
>   As long as you are in it;
> I can shut my eyes and see you,
>   I can think of you every minute.

I am convinced that this was sent to little Victor, and that Victor understood every word of it. That is its triumph. And that is what saves it from being funny. With the likes of Victor as his reader, why should any poet yearn for aesthetic sophistication? Sincerity is enough. There is nothing particularly camp about that.

VERBAL MUSCLE

Jean Genet, *Prisoner of Love* (London: Picador, 1989)

From Jean Genet you would not expect — would you? — a
conventional account of the struggle for Palestine. Although it was
written on the suggestion of Yasser Arafat, and although it is
unvaryingly opposed to Israeli policy and insulting to Hussein of
Jordan, *Prisoner of Love* is as far from pushing a party line as you
could imagine. The result is amazingly sinuous and seductive, an
expansive rhapsody on the fragile composure of virility.

There are many moments when the sheer perversity of Genet's
mind reasserts itself, invoking the most fantastic flights of his
fiction. President Nasser's funeral is likened to the scenes when
footballers embrace after a victory. A statue of the Virgin shows
off her Child as a 'hoodlum' (where have translators been for the
last forty years?) might ostentate his penis. A croupier's inscrutable
expression is likened to that of a man surreptitiously doing up his
flies in public. Schoolboys wield their grenades as though they were
gigantic testicles, primed to go off at any moment. A Jewish funeral
in occupied France reminds Genet of the dispersal of drag queens
through the Bois de Boulogne at dawn.

But this kind of thing does not always work. When Genet
merely speaks of 'a Patriarch devoutly masturbating the shaft of
his golden crozier' one is inevitably disappointed. In the best of his
fiction, he would have had that crozier budding and throbbing for
several tantalising paragraphs, before asperging the congregation's
outstretched tongues with orange blossom. Here, the image is
tetchy and snide, a mundane piece of French anti-clericalism.

If you could decorate a palace, even a palace which doesn't
exist, with language, all the way from the throne-room to the lowest
minions' shithouse, Genet's prose would be the most appropriate
pattern to choose. If your taste is for the verbal equivalent of a
Regency Stripe, your sense of aesthetic order will be severely
affronted by the sheer impropriety of Genet's dementia.

Sometimes he is as sublimely pretentious as his earlier career
led us to expect, but to no real purpose. Consider the moment

when he asks, 'But what if it were true that writing is a lie?' This must have been written during a momentary lapse of concentration. He seems, simply, to have forgotten the main premise of modern literature: that the only kind of truth language can reliably manage is the merely linguistic truth of tautology ('Tomorrow is another day') in which literature aspires to the self-evident fatuity of the equation $1 = 1$. The classic Genet text tends to be far bolder: for it is totally at home in the mendacious and disruptive mathematics of $1 = 6$.

At other times he is, simply, wrong ('English aristocrats and English mechanics alike can all whistle Vivaldi and the songs of sparrows and other English birds') or banal ('Sometimes I wonder whether I didn't live that life especially so that I might arrange its episodes in the same seeming disorder as the images in a dream').

On the other hand, there are moments whose weakness is so extreme that it becomes enchanting. Look at this spurt of uncharacteristic reverence for humanity: 'More and more I believe I exist in order to be the terrain and proof which show other men that life consists in the uninterrupted emotions flowing through all creation. The happiness my hand knows in a boy's hair will be known by another hand, is already known. And although I shall die, that happiness will live on.' If I had said this, it would be banal. The fact that it comes from Jean Genet makes its ordinariness as extravagant as if Doris Day had said *fuck*.

Thus, for *Prisoner of Love* to be even remotely tolerable, one has to respect the writer Genet: to come to it with his other books in mind, yet without expecting their phosphorescent sexual events. One should read it in conjunction with *Funeral Rites*, his other narrative of political rape. That book, Genet's account of the Nazi occupation of Paris, interlocks with this through the familiar image of Hitler stroking a wolfhound: both reassuringly domestic and distinctly threatening. But where the novel was a tortured reworking of sexual events and fantasies, arising at body heat out of the illogic of passion, the present book is more a record of affection, at once cooler and more intense. Unexpectedly, there are even a few good jokes: a boy who catches his father shitting pretends discreetly to have mistaken him for a Norwegian.

As you will have gathered, this is less a political book than a linguistic gymnasium, the sweaty flexarium of Genet's verbal muscle. Despite its concern to relay an accurate impression of the fedayeen and their cause, it keeps calling up literary precedents. Genet says, for instance, that driving into Amman was like entering Haroun al-Rashid's Baghdad in 800 AD. This takes us back to that momentous event in French and gay cultural history, the publication between 1898 and 1904 of J.C.V. Mardrus's 16-volume translation of the *Arabian Nights*.

Although he is conscious of this danger and tries to avoid it, Genet now takes his place among European mytholaters of the 'exotic' east. For this reason I think the book's *force* has *farce* inscribed right the way through it. I would love to know what Arafat thought of it.

SAP AND SINEW

Charley Shively (ed), *Calamus Lovers: Walt Whitman's Working-Class Camerados* (San Francisco: Gay Sunshine, 1989)

Walt Whitman was a collector of boys. His notebooks are full of them: their names, ages and occupations, the subjects of his conversations with them, fragments of physical detail: 'tall, well-tann'd', 'a great head of brown yellowy shining hair thick & longish', 'tall & slender', 'red hair', 'young slight fair feminine', 'blonde', 'rough', 'tall, sandy, young', and so on. And a number of these short notes come to the same happy conclusion: 'slept with me Sept 3d', 'slept with me', 'slept with him Dec 4th '62', 'slept with me last night weather soft, cool enough, warm enough, heavenly'.

Of course, we are speaking of a period when beds were more routinely shared than now, when men and boys swam naked together without fear of arrest, and when the age of consent in most of the United States was 10. But the relaxed way in which all of this was generally accepted changed during Whitman's lifetime: the Brooklyn police started harassing bathers, for instance, and we know that the poet eventually gained a reputation in Camden as a 'lecherous old man'.

The American poet Charley Shively has gathered in this one volume enough letters to and from the Good Gay Poet to remind us that many of the boys the biographers refer to as his friends were actually his boyfriends. Included here are Fred Vaughan, the Union soldiers Tom Sawyer and Lewy Brown, tram-conductor Peter Doyle, Harry Stafford, Bill Duckett and many more, who have tended to be downgraded or completely overlooked in the biographies. (Vaughan, according to Shively the inspirer of the homo-erotic 'Calamus' poems, is not even mentioned in Justin Kaplan's 1980 life of Whitman.)

Shively's approach to the material is uncompromising. He starts from a premise with which I am broadly in sympathy: 'Those who begin with the soul (New England transcendentals quite notably) will never find any soul. Whitman entered the gates of ecstasy through both his and his partner's mouth and cock'. Quite so, and it needed to be said. But there are times when Shively's outspokenness militates against the solidity of his arguments. He is often a lot more excited by the letters he is introducing than they turn out to warrant. Furthermore, while I accept that a certain amount of wishful thinking is a necessary part of all polemical logic, to say that 'Every time a boy gets his cock sucked a bird sings in Walt's throat' adds nothing to our understanding of the gulf between Whitman's time and our own. Even Shively's jokes defy logic. At one point he says 'Cocksucking and bathing go together. Doubtless bathing itself is an invention of cocksuckers'. Surely, the opposite would be just as funny and far more accurate.

Some of the most touching material concerns the poet's relationship with Harry Stafford, who was a teenager when Whitman was in his late fifties. They spent several years together, on and off, in an intimacy that Whitman was reluctant to interrupt even when staying in other people's houses: 'My (adopted) son, a young man of 18, is with me now . . . Could I bring him with me, to share my room, & your hospitality & be with me?' 'My nephew & I when traveling always share the same room together & the same bed'. 'Should like to fetch my boy Harry Stafford with me, as he is in my convoy like — We occupy the same room & bed —'

Harry had a fiery temper which led to countless separations. A ring which Whitman gave him was taken back and re-given several times in 1876 and '77. But even if this ritual became routine, the youth certainly did not lose sight of the ring's intense significance. He wrote to Whitman in November 1877: 'I wish you would put the ring on my finger again, it seems to me there is something that is wanting to compleete our friendship when I am with you. I have tride to studdy it out but cannot find out what it is. You know when you put it on there was but one thing to part it from me and that was death' [sic].

Whenever they stayed at the Stafford family's farm near Timber Creek, the two lovers would spend as much time as they could bathing and sunbathing together, naked on a secluded stretch of the creek. In a letter to Anne Gilchrist dated 22 February 1876, Whitman wrote: 'At least two hours forenoon, & two afternoon, down by the *creek* — Passed between *sauntering* — the *hickory saplings* — & *"Honor* is the *subject* of my story"'. It has been suggested that Whitman is writing in code here, and that hickory-saplings and honor-subject mean H.S.: Harry Stafford.

If so, it is not at all excessive for Charley Shively to say that this passage in the published version of *Specimen Days*, dated 5

September 1877, is richly erotic: '. . . daily and simple exercise I am fond of — to pull on that young hickory sapling out there — to sway and yield to its tough-limber upright stem — haply to get into my old sinews some of its elastic fibre and clear sap . . . At other spots convenient I have selected, besides the hickory just named, strong and limber boughs of beech or holly . . . for my natural gymnasia, for arms, chest, can soon feel the sap and sinew rising through me, like mercury to heat. I hold on boughs or slender trees caressingly there in the sun and shade, wrestle with their innocent stalwartness — and *know* the virtue thereof passes from them into me'. Of course, if the hickory sapling is Harry Stafford, we may legitimately begin to question the identities of beech and holly, not to mention all those other 'boughs or slender trees'.

Whitman clearly saw such relationships as conducive to the spiritual and physical good health of both partners: for, as he wrote on 28 March 1879, 'I tell you Harry, it is the *stomach, belly* & liver that make the principal foundation of all *feeling well — with one other thing*'. This other organ is the one that received so much attention and exercise on the bank of the creek. Looking back later (28 February 1881) he went so far as to assert to the boy: 'I realize plainly that *if I had not known you* — if it hadn't been for you & our friendship & my going down there summers to the creek with you — and living there with your folks, & the kindness of your mother, & cheering me up — I believe *I should not be a living man to-day*'.

Other gems printed here include a letter to the poet from a soldier called Nicholas Palmer, apparently seeking information on how to get work in a brothel; Whitman did not reply, but kept the letter and attached a note to it: 'I itch to satisfy my curiosity as to what this young man can have really taken me for'. Few itches in the tantalising history of regret can really have required so little scratching.

Charley Shively has a healthy contempt for academics — as anyone must who has ever had to read the drivel, either simple-minded or downright deceitful, with which American scholars have stifled the voices of their two greatest Nineteenth Century poets, Whitman and Emily Dickinson. Shively considers his own status as gay poet more than enough qualification to speak with authority on Whitman. His own sex life is occasionally — and quite gratuitously — introduced as proud evidence on Whitman's behalf, as in this passage: 'Whitman also describes cruising Lafayette Park, the area opposite the White House, where I myself sucked a passing stranger's cock on a bench over a hundred years later'.

At one point Shively says the Chinese had the right idea during the Cultural Revolution: send the professors into the fields for a bit of hard labour. This *yah-boo-sucks* attitude to scholarship won't earn him any brownie points with the Ivy League faculties, but it does give the book a breath-taking zest which is alternately funny and irritating. After all, his own task is not so very far from the academics', and its execution has involved him in a lot of perfectly conventional research. To protest otherwise is futile: a bit like spitting in the mirror.

Appended to the letters is a generous selection (59 in all) of Whitman's homo-erotic poems, which remind us, if we had forgotten, of the point of what has preceded them. They are printed with the original pronouns restored. It is so *obvious* from the poems where Whitman's erotic interests lay ('Manhood balanced and florid and full! / My lovers suffocate me!'), that one is inclined to gasp again at the sheer *chutzpah* of the critics who either ignore the erotic issue or try to wriggle their way out of it by speaking blandly of platonic friendships. The material included in *Calamus Lovers* should put a stop to all this nonsense; but it will not.

POISONED PEN

Juan Goytisolo, *Marks of Identity* and *Landscapes After the Battle*
(London: Serpent's Tail, 1988)

Juan Goytisolo was born in Barcelona in 1931; he emigrated to
France in 1957. These two facts locate him as a writer, historically
as well as geographically. His childhood straddles the Civil War,
his adulthood the years of Franco's 'peace', the migration of
unemployed Spaniards northwards and of northern tourists
southwards, Franco's death, the restoration of democracy and
the monarchy (if the two can really be said to co-exist) and Spain's
triumphant entry into the European Community. Goytisolo views
all of this, from his position as Spaniard and exile and 'European',
with a jaundiced gaze and a poisoned pen.

Already in *Fiestas* (1958) Goytisolo was robustly anti-fascist
and anti-Catholic, and deeply concerned about the treatment of
racial minorities and migrant workers in Spain. Already he was
concerned at the murderousness of heterosexual paedophilia.
What was not then apparent, in a book with a relatively
straightforward plot and cast of characters, was the extent to
which he would later use the fictive process itself to convey his
view of European cultural catastrophe.

In *Marks of Identity* (1966), which is the first part of a trilogy,
Alvaro Mendiola returns to Spain after long exile and revisits
some of the scenes of his earlier life. Consulting them and a whole
sequence of documents and snapshots (the 'marks' in the title),
he tries retrospectively to piece together his own life, as if personal
identity could be captured in an orderly arrangement of
souvenirs.

But Alvaro's search is as much for Spain's identity as for
his own. He laments — as Goytisolo, too, laments — the price
at which Franco won his economic 'miracle': the systematic
brutality of his regime, and (perhaps of even more lasting ill-
effect) his indiscriminate encouragement of tourism, which led
to an annual influx of ten million northern Europeans by the
mid-Sixties. There is a horrific scene at the end of *Marks of
Identity* when Alvaro revisits Barcelona and watches tourists
swarming ignorantly over the castle which the guide books
present as a monument to peace, but which was actually once
one of Spain's most notorious jails, where countless Republicans

were shot. If this cultural rape is not an abdication of sovereignty (that great terror of Europe's right wingers) what is?

All of this is narrated in an appropriate disorder whose first victim is chronology. Alvaro's quest takes shape as an incomplete jigsaw of retrieval from a past already too confused to be resolvable into lucid history. Following Modernism's conviction that the century itself is not lucid, Goytisolo's fiction recreates in the reader a sense of powerlessness in the face of disorientation and menace. At the moments when you are most in need of clear information, it torments you with further confusion.

Although gay, Goytisolo is not what you would call a 'gay novelist'. Only the occasional character is homosexual: in *Fiestas* two characters converse at hilarious cross purposes, one believing he is making a secret political contact, the other just as sure he is being picked up; in *Marks of Identity* a mother courts an apparently timid musician in his fifties, only to see him run off with her 18 year-old son. Nor do I think there is a 'gay sensibility' (a concept which, anyway, I profoundly mistrust) in operation here. Sure, the author speaks as an outsider; but, given his history, he would do so whether he were gay or straight. In any case, he seems to have other, more pressing concerns.

As his career has progressed, Goytisolo has become increasingly interested in the Arabic cultures, both as expressed in triumphant 'Moorish' influences on Spanish life, and as now found among disadvantaged Algerian immigrants and migrant workers in Paris. Needless to say, this interest has turned his attention to the matter of racial discrimination, one of the main themes of *Landscapes After the Battle* (1983).

Racism is, perhaps, *the* major issue of our times, certainly in Europe since the Holocaust and the 'granting' of Independence to so many developing nations after the Second World War. To some considerable, but still limited, extent, this has been reflected in Western Modernist literature: Proust on the Dreyfus case, Joyce on Bloom, Faulkner on Dixie, Pound on usury, and so on. Goytisolo approaches the subject, with a touch of venom and a nasty sense of humour.

Landscapes is a demented book, inspired by the spirit of panic. Paris gets the William Burroughs treatment, without the boy-boy sex. If it has a single subject it is the watering down of European culture to a dribble of white blandness. There is a running joke about Julio Iglesias; or rather, Iglesias is presented as the joke itself. This grinning paragon of 'easy listening' is what

Spanish culture has come to in the European Community: regular teeth, a good sun tan (but not too dark) and songs sufficiently lacking in commitment to cross frontiers and still sell. All the more meaningful, therefore, the author's photo at the end of *Marks of Identity*: the balding Goytisolo stands, looking shifty, in front of a poster of the Iglesias grin.

The novels we in Britain are most used to in translation from Spanish are Latin American monsters of 'magical realism' by writers like Marquez. Do not expect equivalent gymnastics of the imagination from Goytisolo. His books are not particularly deeply imagined. His characters do not exactly leap from the page — as we like to imagine they do in, say, Dickens. That kind of detailed psychological inventiveness does not really seem to be Goytisolo's forte; nor, for that matter, his concern.

His commitment to Post-Modernist tricksiness is yawn-inducing at times. But what prevents both of these books' disappearing up their own avant-garde arses is the strength of their social commitment; and any aesthetic judgement we make on them must be connected with the extent to which Goytisolo's artistry manages to convey his political drift. There is little point in reading him as a 'mere' novelist.

Juan Goytisolo, *Count Julian* (London: Serpent's Tail, 1989)

This novel is the second volume of the trilogy which *Marks of Identity* began. *Count Julian* seems better, because shorter and tauter. But you must decide for yourself: either you like a novel without narrative, or you don't. Either you prefer the doings of language to those of fictional characters, or you don't. A great verbal stylist chooses not to beguile and charm, but to disgust and affront: you are either enchanted or bored. An anti-sexist and anti-racist homosexual novelist writes an outspokenly sexist, racist and homophobic text: you either try to understand what he is doing or you snap the book shut and fling it out of the window. The choice is yours.

As usual, Goytisolo is concerned to expose and deplore the depths to which Spain has sunk since the civil war that brought Franco to power. He is in no mood to compromise with any of the beneficiaries of fascism. Everything they do and stand for is tainted. The great literary classics of Spain are shown to be useful for squashing insects with, and then, not surprisingly, found to be full of squashed insects. Later in the book, Spanish culture is attacked by a swarm of bluebottles, for all the world as though it were a succulent turd. What else, the author asks, can one expect from a nation addicted to chick-peas?

Count Julian acts out the racism and sexism of the Spanish middle class. It is intended as both an affront to their sense of decorum and confirmation of their most lurid fears. Goytisolo presents Arabs as a horde of invasive rapists with huge cocks. 'I offer you my country, invade it, sack it, plunder it.' With such entreaties as these, he offers Spain to the Arabs, thereby stirring the deepest terror of those who will never read him, his nation's bourgeoisie.

So I suppose you have to be a Catholic fascist to get the full effect of the book and its author's rage. Speaking personally, my own appetite for literature is so jaded that I no longer (or did I ever?) find shocking a scene in which a naked nun flagellates herself in worship of 'the Omnipresent' General Franco. Indeed, I find the idea obvious and, frankly, a little dull. And perhaps you have to be a Spanish man, *muy macho*, to be affronted by Goytisolo's repeated taunts that Spaniards have pricks as limp as lettuce leaves, while the Arabs are blessed with sumptuous serpents. You certainly have to be someone I am not to appreciate the book's strident vaginophobia.

In Goytisolo's remorselessly nasty rewrite of Little Red Riding Hood, the little girl is replaced by a saintly Spanish boy, the Big Bad Wolf by a Moor; the latter, of course, rapes and kills the former. When the rewrite is itself rewritten, the boy is seduced into committing suicide by his humiliating desire for the Moor's 'snake'. A magnificent scene, thoroughly perverting the Indian Rope Trick, has the boy hanging himself while watching the snake rear up. This, I have to say, is splendid stuff. Objectionable it may be; but I would happily swap what shreds of virtue I have left for the ability to write like this.

It follows that the book's true hero is the Spanish language. Needless to say, it doesn't put in an appearance here; but this translation is easily good enough to give us a strong flavour of the original's symphonic quality, especially during its climax and dying fall. But be warned. This symphony, even if it has its soporific passages, is no lullaby. Bring earplugs.

FEDERICO'S REVENGE

Lluís Fernàndez, *The Naked Anarchist* (London: GMP, 1990)

Aurelio Santonja is in exile in Amsterdam. His friends, a mad gaggle of Valencian queens, write letters to him to keep him in touch with their own triumphs and each other's pratfalls. In a knotted rope of gossip, love and malice intertwine.

The sense of sex as sin; the idea that all men are available to a man in drag; the belief that the move from gay man to drag queen to transsexual to woman is an uncomplicated continuum — all of this is part of the book's characteristically Mediterranean flavour. It also places the book firmly in the era of its first publication, 1979.

As in so much pre-AIDS literature, there is a careless association of sex and death — partly, no doubt, derived from Fernandez's reading of William Burroughs. He is not as good as Burroughs at the revolting set-piece of sexual indulgence. But there are some very good, and often funny, scenes here. I was particularly tickled by an account of screwing during an orchestral concert, and by the tale of a fishmonger who castrates her gay son.

For all its attempts to be stylish, the novel is packed with extraordinary lapses. I quote a handful. 'Wearing a belt with a military buckle, his shirt was undone to the navel'; 'us queens were vying for attention'; 'the less words exchanged the better'; 'Everyone, apart from the indefatigable Momy Von, of course, are asleep in their rooms'; 'he pawed her cruelly, like a cat plays with its prey'.

I am going to be generous, and assume that such faults are deliberate: let them represent the necessary tackiness of queendom, the unforgiveable but inevitable ladder in a stocking. There are, however, other problems with this translation. So awkward is the transatlantic vocabulary that, at one point, a pair of buns becomes 'a pair of bums'. And what is a 'yachting club'?

One day *The Naked Anarchist* may take its place in Spanish literary history as a letting off of steam in that short but exiting period between Franco's death and the AIDS catastrophe. What we have here is, in effect, an assertion of gay presence, every bit as rude and effortfully beautiful as the queens it describes; but duller. To be reading such a raucous sigh of relief at the demise of Francisco Franco in the weeks after the unseating of Margaret Thatcher does, to be sure, constitute a special, peripheral pleasure.

This is the flip-side of Lorca — and I mean flip. A virulent, wasting strain of verbal diarrhoea, one might call it Federico's Revenge.

DANCING WITH CONVICTS

Harold Norse, *Memoirs of a Bastard Angel* (London: Bloomsbury, 1990)

Any man who was chatted up by Marlon Brando in 1944 but let him get away really is under an obligation to explain how he ever managed to forgive himself. So there has been a definite need for a Harold Norse autobiography for some time. Well, here it is, presented as 'A Fifty-Year Literary and Erotic Odyssey'. If a book-worthy life consists of countless encounters with famous people, alternating with even more countless encounters with the bodies of anonymous strangers, Norse's life cannot fail to make interesting reading.

Norse was Chester Kallman's boyfriend when W.H. Auden arrived in America to steal the boy away. Norse knew a poor black boy called James Baldwin, who was trying to become a writer; he read the homosexually explicit manuscript of Baldwin's *Go Tell It on the Mountain* long before it was published in watered-down form. Norse read the manuscript of *The Glass Menagerie* the day after Tennessee Williams completed it. Norse was the first writer Allen Ginsberg ever met — a week before Jack Kerouac, a fortnight before William Burroughs. Norse was reduced to impotence by an unwanted assault on his penis by W.H. Auden's teeth.

Norse resisted the charms of Paul Goodman and Gore Vidal, in addition to Brando. Norse helped entertain Dylan Thomas on his notorious visit to New York. Norse knew and was often praised by William Carlos Williams. Norse could not prise more than a few brief sentences out of Pier Paolo Pasolini. Norse was instrumental in William Burroughs' development of the cut-up technique in fiction. Idries Shah cured Norse's homosexuality, but Norse caught the bug again only minutes later from a peasant boy at the roadside. And so on.

Much of this is fascinating stuff, and should have made this one of the most interesting books of the year. But something has gone badly wrong. Firstly, all the name-dropping, though impressive enough, can do nothing to drown out the sound of Norse's own name. He uses most of the big names to reflect glory on his own. There is an egotism here, stemming from resentment at what he perceives as the failure of his own literary reputation, that becomes boring. He is forever quoting other poets' praise of his own work; even the slightest compliment, oral or written, from forty years ago is remembered, or reinvented, and duly noted down.

The second major problem is that Norse does not write prose very well. This is a real disappointment. Readers of his poetry will be used to a much more pithy, concrete and — let's face it — intelligent idiom. Too often, here, Norse resorts to cracker-barrel banalities: 'with the passage of time I learned that tact spares feelings', 'great wealth shelters one from all but flattery', 'the Muse works in mysterious ways', 'What a precarious calling poetry was!'. Truly wonderful sequences of events lead to the most crushingly dull conclusions: 'Dancing with convicts on a prison island and meeting the Duke of Windsor did not happen every day.' This tendency to drain the interest from the interesting occurs, too, in his literary judgements. Of Tennessee Williams, Norse says: 'beneath this ineffectual exterior there lurked a literary giant'. And, of *The Glass Menagerie:* 'It was a masterpiece'. I can find this kind of thing in *Reader's Digest.* I don't expect to find it in a literate literary memoir.

Even on poetry, his own field, Norse can go wildly wrong. Just after mentioning Hart Crane's *The Bridge*, a poem written very much under the influence of Eliot's *The Waste Land*, he says Eliot's poem was 'no model for succeeding generations — like Pound's *Cantos*, it was too hermetic'. This astonishing remark makes one think Norse has completely overlooked the recent poetic history of his own country, let alone of ours. I accept that Norse dislikes Pound for some very good reasons — such as his fascism — but to deny Pound's influence, especially, is a bit like an environmentalist trying to pretend that the internal combustion engine has had no effect on modern life.

Still, let me end on a more upbeat note. *Bastard Angel* is, in spite of everything, well worth reading. For all its faults, it is fascinating on Auden's early years in America; and, for all his, Norse is the genial host of a party at which, although the drinks run out early, lots of strange people have turned up. You never know what might happen next. If you attend it you may be disappointed; but if you miss the party altogether, you'll be furious.

PATRICK WHITE (1912-1990)

The obituaries called him cantankerous. Could this be, by any chance, because he was left wing and hated the press? Could it be because his novels, although poetic and profound, are also political? Radio 3's 'Kaleidoscope' said he had a chip on his shoulder about you-know-what. Well, it's just as well he did; otherwise, he might not have bothered writing about it. Living with a 'Dago', his Greek lover Manoly Lascaris, sensitised him to the pervasive presence of racism in everyday life; living as a gay man — and, just as bad, a writer — among Australian men undermined any sense he might otherwise have had of belonging to his own nation.

His fiction, fully informed by the techniques and concerns of Modernism, is always daring. White is at his best when stretching himself: in *A Fringe of Leaves*, for instance, by entering the mind of a white woman in the 19th Century, and then, after a shipwreck, having her integrated into an aborigine community; in *The Solid Mandala*, by representing the kind of simple-mindedness that some would call madness, but which White sees as having access to its own unique profundities; or in *The Vivisector*, his 'portrait of the artist', when he takes as his subject a painter with an almost entirely visual imagination, unlike his own intellect.

White was never satisfied; he always strove for new effects. The result is that when he fails, he fails grandly. Most people rest his reputation on *Voss*, but there is so much more to his work. I treasure *Riders in the Chariot* as a rare — scandalously rare — example of a novel that is self-evidently eligible for the stakes of 'greatness', but nevertheless addresses issues like homophobia and racism, and addresses them both at its centre and in depth. Perhaps not since Proust has anyone so conspicuously achieved this balance. It is a great novel that is also a great political novel.

A tragedy modelled on the myth of Christ, *Riders in the Chariot* tells the life story of Mordecai Himmelfarb, who survives the Holocaust in Europe, and emigrates, only to be crucified (more or less literally) by Australian racism. His Evangelist, the recorder of his Passion, is a young aborigine, the painter and outcast Alf Dubbo. By building a relationship between these two characters, White proposes a serious comparison between Nazi treatment of Jews and white Australian dispossession and extermination of the aborigines. It works.

The Twyborn Affair magically (or, perhaps, just eccentricly) chronicles the life of the trans-sexual Eudoxia/Eddie/Eadith, sometime jackaroo on a remote Australian farm (where he goes to prove his manhood, and is raped to prove another man's) and brothel madam in phoney-wartime London. This exploration of femininity and effeminacy, like so much gay culture, tells us far more about the fragile construction of masculinity than any number of John Wayne — or, for that matter, Paul Hogan — films.

In opposition to the philistinism of Australian life and culture, White worked in the medium of an elegant weirdness that called everything into question: not only the 'universal' and 'metaphysical' issues that the liberal tradition requires of great art — questions of 'the meaning of life' — but also the structures that shape the daily lives of both ordinary and extraordinary people. He wrote a kind of metaphysical melodrama that was, at the same time, committed.

He did not write out of love for all humanity. His humanism stopped short of sympathy for narrow-mindedness: his books contain many minor characters who are represented as being little better than stupid. He wrote them, I feel, out of as much contempt as amusement, and they generally get up to no good. They accidentally or maliciously cause harm to others, and never attain anything like the degree of enlightenment that could pierce their complacency.

Like so many of his generation, White paid his patriotic dues: he was an RAF Intelligence Officer in the Middle East (where he met Manoly Lascaris) during the 1939-45 war. This did not mean he was a compliant subject, and in later years he took vociferous and active stands on many issues. He demanded the restoration of substantial tracts of Australia to the aborigines. He was vigorously opposed to the use of the Pacific as a nuclear testing-ground. He refused to attend the Bicentennial celebrations, calling their organisers 'vulgar Philistines' and notoriously referring to Charles and Diana Windsor as 'royal goons'.

When White was awarded the Nobel Prize for Literature in 1973, a callow journalist referred to Manoly Lascaris as his 'companion'. White fired off an angry letter at once, saying the correct word was 'lover'. To someone for whom words were at the heart of what mattered, frankness ('bluntness', some would call it, or 'bloody-mindedness') was the very root of personal and social integrity. So long as they read his books, he didn't give a fuck what people thought of him.

JUST SAY NOTHING

John Strang and Gerry Stimson (Eds), *AIDS and Drug Misuse: The Challenge for Policy and Practice in the 1990s* (London: Routledge, 1990)

There are up to two and a half million people, worldwide, injecting drugs for 'non-medicinal purposes'. This book addresses a broad range of issues relating to the HIV epidemic within that group.

The book contains work by 35 contributors, all of whom have 'international reputations in their fields'. Only 6 of them (or possibly 7) are women, none of whom contributes an article written on her own or in collaboration with other women without men. The drug users themselves — unless their presence is hidden among the professional specialists — have not been invited to take part.

I do not necessarily mean this as a blanket criticism, but it does tend to signal the kind of book we can expect. The language the essayists use is another major indicator. False notes keep creeping in as a result of the effort to write 'serious', 'detached', 'professional' English.

Typical of the 'scientific' approach is a sentence in the editors' introduction: 'We are privileged that as a result of modern scientific study and communication we are well informed at a point in the HIV crisis when we have great opportunity to influence the unfolding course of the epidemic'. Though presumably not meant as such, this sounds suspiciously like careerism. At the very least, it is thoughtless.

One writer, when trying to describe typical reactions of a prisoner to the discovery that he is HIV-positive, conjures up the following: 'If I am seropositive, I don't care whom I infect.' The prisoner may become morally confused, but at least he will still care about the correctness of his grammar and medical terms.

Because of the pressure to sound 'objective', some writers are still being remarkably tentative in their recommendations. One of the conclusions of an essay on the 'neuropsychiatric complications' of HIV infection is that 'Highly confrontational and restrictive approaches [of professional treatment] may need to be replaced by more supportive and individually tailored programmes.' *May* they? All the evidence elsewhere in the book screams out that they *must*.

Understatement is obviously considered a professional necessity. Hence the appearance of bland sentences like this: 'ethical and scientific standards in the control of HIV and care of AIDS in prison do not correspond to those accepted for the community in general'. There is murder being committed in our prisons on a massive scale — and it is not being committed by the prisoners. To be speaking of 'standards' at all seems beside the point.

Moreover, for all the book's efforts to cover a very wide field of issues, it has some conspicuous omissions. For example, it contains few references to racial issues; and none are indexed. For another example, an article on the drug scene in Italy fails even to mention the Roman Catholic Church, let alone the Mafia (or the Camorra or n'Dranghetta).

Other controversial issues are also skimmed over. One fleeting sentence mentions that 'The world's pharmaceutical industries have a partial responsibility for the unfolding of trends in illicit drug use, in that many mind-altering pharmaceutical products eventually find a niche in the illegal market'. I suppose there is a whole new book to be written on that morally murky topic. All I know is that, whenever anyone says 'drug misuse' or 'drug abuse', I think of Burroughs Wellcome.

As far as I can recall, no essay mentions the heavy responsibility that politicians in the developed world must bear for turning the 'third' world into a vast gimcrack laboratory for the production of drugs. Nor is there any political analysis, here, of the responsibility for the poverty that so many of the essayists see as having a direct influence, firstly on levels of drug use, and then on levels of *unsafe* drug use.

One or two myths continue to be peddled about gay men. In an essay on communication and education, we are told that 'Male gay culture has a self-confessed history of promiscuity — but that history has been thrown into sharp relief by the strength of the struggle to save lives and rebuild the community in a more settled and caring form'. The phrase 'self-confessed' shows that the writers have not bothered to find out what 'promiscuity' has meant to gay men. The second half of the sentence shows no awareness of what we have managed to do in our remarkably successful experiment with safer — but often no less 'promiscuous' — forms of sex.

The author of the article on prisons says that oral and anal sex occur 'rather frequently' in men's prisons, 'even between prisoners who have heterosexual orientation outside prison'. He cites as evidence an American report that '19 per cent of prisoners serving sentences of six months or over report at least one homosexual contact while in prison'. This does not seem 'rather' frequent at all. Indeed, it strikes me as bordering on rarity. I wonder if the evidence is reliable.

On the other hand, an essay on models of self-help for HIV-positive drug users is right to criticise gay-related responses to users. Negative stereotypes of crazy, criminal junkies, unable to make decisions for themselves, are clearly unhelpful. But blithe libertarian attitudes are not much better: 'Telling someone who feels compelled to inject themselves with powerful substances that it is their right to do so and that their lifestyle is as valid as any other ... does not help clients to overcome what any objective observer would see as a problem'. Apart from this genuflection to the god Objectivity (who, as any atheist knows, does not exist), this is well said.

Even without AIDS, there is a massive health problem among drug users. Deaths by drug-related violence and suicide, or by accidental overdose, still greatly outnumber AIDS-related deaths. Moreover, for many users — as the essay on the crisis in Italy says — every injection is 'a symbolic challenge to death'. This obviously has complex implications for health educators.

So does an apparent disagreement among the experts. While one essay here claims that 'The drug injector is now seen as a rational actor, who will respond to public health information', another states bluntly that 'Education does not work as a means of prevention of illegal drug use'. (I realise that these two statements are not necessarily contradictory, but their implications seem to be.)

In any case, the public services are often pulling in opposite directions. This is most obvious in relation to the provision of needles and other works: while drug workers are trying to arrange needle exchanges, police and politicians are often involved in trying to stamp out drug use altogether, by ensuring that as few syringes as possible reach the injectors.

Not that the provision of sterile needles is necessarily a solution. In much of Italy, for instance, cheap works are available all round the clock at pharmacies and supermarkets; but needle sharing has continued. (I have lost count of the number of times I have seen boys sharing disposables in the back streets of Naples and Salerno and then discarding them on the ground.) Like jacking off, jacking up is often seen as an activity best indulged in *à deux;* the trouble is that, once friends are close enough to do the former — which, as we all know, is both congenial and safe — they often infer that to refuse to do the latter would be a betrayal of that very same friendship.

Sharing needles is not, of course, the only problem. While drug users in the UK and USA have been, by and large, quite amenable to changing their injecting habits — particularly in the context of well-organised but not coercive needle-exchange schemes — they have proved much less willing to alter their heterosexual behaviour. As one essayist puts it, 'HIV may now be recognisably a sexually transmitted disease amongst injecting drug users'. An unexpected consequence of this fact is that 'the greatest natural boundary to the future spread of HIV in the United States is sexual segregation by age'. Ageism has its uses, after all.

One of these essays rightly asserts — and other essays confirm — that 'HIV antibody status is more important than drug use status. In consequence, services should be matched to the HIV problem first, with drug use placed second'. The message is clear: 'Politicians may have to decide which is the main priority, the fight against drugs or the fight against HIV.' (There goes that word 'may' again.) In many cases, politicians seem to have shared Nancy Reagan's ridiculously ill-informed slogan JUST SAY NO. Worse still, following the example of Nancy's demented spouse, many amended this to JUST SAY NOTHING.

It does not help if a book of this kind then compounds the fault, in its apparent belief that academic respectability requires a measure of discretion. Nor, for that matter, does the cover design exactly help. It consists of a map of the world. Taking pride of place beside the title is — Africa.

COPING WITH LOSS

David Robilliard, *Baby Lies Truthfully* (London, Inanout Press, 1990)

One of the purposes of poetry is to cope with loss. I've always believed — and this may be only symbolically rather than literally true — that the world's first poems were inscriptions on gravestones. Certainly, the *Greek Anthology* is full of epitaphs which pithily, and often humorously, express the commemorative imperative: the need to mark a loved one's death.

Certainly, too, some of the most emotionally expressive homo-erotic literature to have passed down to us from the ancient world has taken the form of personal laments: those of Gilgamesh for Enkidu, Achilles for Patroclus, David for Jonathan. (This is partly due to the fact that male-male affairs with happy endings have rarely survived the censor's scissors. Only those which ended in death were acceptable.)

A long string of funeral elegies connects the literature of classical Greece with that of our own world. Milton's *Lycidas*, Shelley's *Adonais*, Arnold's *Thyrsis* and Tennyson's *In Memoriam* — all marking the deaths of male friends — stand at the very centre of the so-called 'mainstream' of English verse, refusing to be marginalised. And the most conspicuously 'Modern' of modern poems, *The Waste Land*, is in part Eliot's attempt to come to terms with the death of his beloved friend Jean Verdenal, who was killed in the First World War.

Implicit in all creative writing about AIDS are questions which have been asked before, whenever people have died. They were asked again, with a deeper sense of bewilderment, in the first waves of literature about the Holocaust. What can I say? Why say anything? Isn't art trivial when compared with death? AIDS literature is often approaching the point at which it gives itself up as a bad job: trivial, redundant, irrelevant.

But there always comes an important point at which the artist thinks: No, I will not be silenced, I must say *something*, anything. Silence = Death. Art's main purpose must be to make that initial break with grieving silence. As Linda Loman says in Arthur Miller's *Death of a Salesman*, 'attention must be paid'.

So, while it no longer seems important to 'immortalise' the dead (which is what poets like Milton and Shelley were trying to do), it is still vital to keep their memory alive for as long as we who knew them continue living. This is true for our sakes at least as much as for theirs.

Poets, of course, can commemorate their friends. But they must also, generally, leave the words by which they themselves will be remembered. This is, perhaps, a more difficult task.

The late David Robilliard's book of poems and drawings *Baby Lies Truthfully*, according its biographical note, 'marks the publication of the first of the poems to chronicle his battle with AIDS'. It is not in the conventional sense a chronicle at all; it says too little. The poems are very short, often little more than fragments of a single idea. But Robilliard seems to have believed that a little is enough. The irony is, I think, that he overdoes the brevity: there are too many gnomic little utterances, and they never cohere into a whole text. For me, his line drawings of faces are often more eloquent.

However, certain individual items gain everything by their refusal to expand. A poem called 'Memory of a Friend', for instance, goes as follows:

> A burst of tears
> from all your friends
> the end

(with no final fullstop). Nothing could be further than this from the massive *In Memoriam*. From the *Greek Anthology* to the personal columns of the local newspaper, among the most effective ways of recording death and grief are the shortest. It is in the rhymes in the personal ads that we find how 'high' culture has permeated 'down' to popular culture to perform a real role of consolation. And better than all of the published war poetry of the First World War, it seems to me, was the message which some anonymous squaddie scrawled on a board above a corpse:

> Sleep on, Beloved Brother;
> Take thy Gentle Rest.

BEING ADMIRED

Jean Cocteau, *Past Tense: The Cocteau Diaries* (London: Methuen, 1990)

Jean Cocteau thought that to publish your journal in your own lifetime — as André Gide had done — was absurd. 'A journal exists only if you put into it, without reservations, everything that occurs to you.' You must hide nothing. 'A journal has to be published posthumously.'

But don't read this volume (which covers the year 1953) in the hope of finding your way into Cocteau's boudoir, let alone his psyche or soul. Although he claims to be 'gossiping to myself here', it is as if he is speaking on a phone line that he knows is being tapped. He is writing for posthumous publication, and is being no more frank than Gide was. As in all his other work, he is writing to create an effect.

Cocteau's narcissism was never introverted. Unlike Narcissus, he needed an audience. If ever he looked in a mirror — and he often did — it was to admire himself, of course, but to admire himself *being admired*. In such clauses as 'if you are reading this diary after my death', you can hear Cocteau's confidence in his own artistic survival. He is like an American President, making sure of his place in history by building a museum dedicated to himself.

There is, of course, much to be admired; he was right about that. While compiling his *Oeuvres complètes*, he suddenly remembered books he had forgotten he wrote. He was massively prolific: in poetry, painting, graphic design, film, theatre, fiction, not to mention an unceasing stream of articles on anything under the sun. While he considered himself an expert on everything, what he seems to have enjoyed best was to build up the reputations of his friends and to demolish those of his enemies.

So, although, at one point, he claims to be far more interested in poetry than in gossip, he does satisfy the reader's curiosity with some fine nuggets of scandal. There is a pathetic account, received first-hand from Vaslav Nijinsky, of Auguste Rodin sculpting the dancer's back. On two consecutive days Nijinsky turns round at the wrong moment. On the first, Rodin has fallen asleep; on the second, he is masturbating.

In a later entry, Cocteau describes a visit from Henri de Montherlant and Roger Peyrefitte, the authors of the paedophile classics *La Ville dont le Prince est un enfant* and *Les Amitiés Particulières* respectively, and at that time 'intimate friends'. 'Whenever a group of lycée boys passed under the arcades, they rushed to the window, where I saw nothing more than their two behinds.' There is a certain gleeful malice involved in this recording of their regal posteriors for posterity.

On 28 August he begins a sentence, 'If I were capable of pride . . .', and on 14 November he says, 'If I were subject to pride . . .' The very words *ooze* vanity, and seem quite unironic. When Jean Genet turns up in 'a splendid car' and announces that he now lives in the Ritz at Barcelona, Cocteau admiringly comments on the fact that Genet is not the victim of the writer-as-thief legend he has built up about himself. But Cocteau himself *was* such a victim: he seems entirely taken in by myths he has built up around his own persona. Not that this mattered much, in terms of everyday living: for by 1953, when he was 64, he was rich enough not to need much contact with reality. No wonder he loved Franz Kafka's diary for the fact that it never refers to the First World War.

Cocteau's art is so resolutely confined to surfaces that he never drew anything better than his pornographic line drawings for Genet and for his own *Le Livre Blanc*. He had found the perfect, depthless subject: nothing but the contours of improbably prodigious flesh. This is also why he was so well suited to the medium of film.

I do not mean this as a criticism. Jean Cocteau did things with surfaces that no one else could have dreamt of. While less able writers than himself won the Nobel Prize for their mudlarking in shallow profundity, Cocteau turned himself into the Torvill and Dean of the glistening surface.

And he had the perfect reason for doing so: 'The sleazier the times, the more important to contradict them with luxury work'. I know the feeling.

TRUE NARCISSISM

Camille Paglia, *Sexual Personae: Art and Decadence from Nefertiti to Emily Dickinson* (New Haven and London: Yale University Press, 1990)

Camille Paglia believes that 'criticism has hugely overestimated the centrality of language to western culture' and has 'failed to see the electrifying sign language of images'. Presumably she means literary criticism rather than art history; but this is a characteristic moment of overstatement, in which slapdash use of the term 'criticism' is expected to do service in support of vast generalisation. Elsewhere, Paglia dismisses Chaucer's poetry as having 'too many words'. These are odd claims for a book this size: a book so mesmerised by the sound of its own voice, so reluctant to quote other contemporary witnesses, so under-illustrated.

Boiled down to its essence, Paglia's argument is that it is natural for men to be unnatural (by building ziggurats or writing poems) but unnatural for women. Anatomy is destiny. Nowhere does she question the concept of 'nature', itself one of men's more peculiar edifices. Instead, she takes it on herself to dole out patronising gold stars with startling *sang froid:* 'Mythology's identification of woman with nature is correct'; 'the historical attribution of narcissism to women is another true myth'. Well, it is certainly true in this case.

Following the course of what she perceives as a continuation of paganism through Christian culture, Paglia tracks down in an impressively broad array of cultural documents traces of what she calls 'decadence'. But what does 'decadent' really mean? Unaware that it is a discredited term, entirely dependent on the moral viewpoint of a particular moment in history, Paglia never bothers to define it. Even as long ago as 1976, Martin Green, himself something of a maverick, had to put it in inverted commas in the subtitle of his *Children of the Sun: A Narrative of 'Decadence' in England after 1918*. Nothing has happened since then to make it a safer term.

But history is not Paglia's strong point. She seems to think of it as an impertinence slipped into academic discourse by nit-picking liberals. She unquestioningly applies the concept of 'homosexuality' to the physical relations between men and boys in ancient Greece. Not surprisingly, therefore, she would rather quote the likes of J.Z. Eglinton than Michel Foucault. Nor, I suppose, has she heard of the more recent researches of David M. Halperin. The ease with which she shrugs off the most recent of her sources, K.J. Dover's magisterial *Greek Homosexuality* (1978) is quite breathtaking: 'I depart from sociological rationales for Greek love. For me, aesthetics are primary.' And that's that.

So this is a survey of literary records of the history of what we now call 'sexuality', which pays precious little attention to that history. To say that 'The beautiful boy is homosexuality's greatest contribution to western culture' is not only to overlook heterosexual women's role in parturition, but also to forget that the concept of 'homosexuality' did not exist until 1868.

Paglia rejoices in bringing out all the old saws about gender and sex. For example: 'there is always a feminine element in the beautiful young man of male homosexuality'. (She should watch the porn star Jeff Stryker in action.) Similarly, 'When admiring the sleek body of a woman athlete, I see androgyny, not femaleness'. (She should watch Flo-Jo in action.) Later, she follows Gibbon in stating that 'Rome's sexual disorientation was great theater, but it led to the collapse of paganism'. She follows the tabloid press in her references to AIDS as a consequence of promiscuity. Indeed, she is always following; rarely does she *lead* with a genuinely original idea.

Furthermore, there are some ridiculous lapses of logic, as when she argues that ancient Athens was not a phallocracy because the Greeks liked their penises small. (Has nobody told her that size does not determine performance?)

When she wishes to put forward an argument which even she realises is indefensible, she is quite likely to secure it pre-emptively with a different argument altogether. Here, for instance, is a very compact version of this strategy: 'The lesbian aesthete does not exist. But if there were one, she would have learned from the perverse male mind.' So, just as one is about to put forward the names of women like Natalie Barney or Romaine Brooks, the author dismisses them with the conventionally homophobic accusation, that they are not real women and therefore don't count.

Paglia apparently sees the feminism she despises as consisting of only a single strand of thought. But her ignorance of what that strand consists of is truly disturbing. She believes feminist women have made advances into professional life by concealing the fact that they menstruate and have babies — or as she puts it, 'In its argument with male society, feminism must suppress the monthly evidence of woman's domination by chthonian nature'. She has evidently never read Gloria Steinem or Germaine Greer, or looked at the work of artists like Judy Chicago.

This matter of insufficient reading affects every chapter on material with which I am familiar. Presumably a bibliography will be provided at the end of the threatened second volume. But if one trawls the footnotes to this volume, one finds only four items dating from after 1980. And even these are hardly the latest idea: one is Virginia Woolf's diary, another is Henry James's notebook, the third is a psychoanalytic study of Michelangelo. The fourth is a dictionary entry by a certain Camille Paglia.

If not from scholarly research, then, where does the author find her authority? In bald statement, as if of fact. Here are some examples. 'The most beautiful woman, making herself a perfect stillness, will always turn Gorgon.' 'English literary distinction begins in the Renaissance and is the creation of one man, Edmund Spenser.' 'Freud has no rivals among his successors because they think he wrote science, when in fact he wrote art.' 'Female genitalia are not beautiful by any aesthetic standard.' 'The more negative homosexual experience, the more it belongs to art.' 'Not a shred of evidence supports the existence of matriarchy anywhere in the world at any time.' The sheer pushiness of this voice sounds like Oscar Wilde dispensing epigrams; but where his paradoxes illuminate by disrupting norms, Paglia's voice is trying to shore up the spent authority of a lost age. At worst, she is often, simply, wrong.

Her comments on visual material are no less rash, no more illuminating. To call Donatello's David 'a frozen wet dream' not only does not add anything to the debate; it actually subtracts from it. This kind of trivialisation of gay art is neither clever nor rare. The juxtaposition of pictures of Byron and Elvis Presley says nothing, except that both men had black hair. It is not much more than a design gimmick, like the cover's splicing of the faces of Nefertiti and Emily Dickinson. It certainly has none of the weight of significance that Paglia attributes to it.

The great fallacy at the heart of the book is a confusion of prejudice with inevitability. To show that people have often *believed,* and written, that woman is nature, is far from proving that woman is nature. Paglia's politics are, of course, explicitly reactionary. This explains the passion with which she seeks to re-establish discredited ideas, while at the same time claiming everything she says as brand new. For instance, to challenge Marxist orthodoxy with the orthodoxy that preceded it does not strike me as moving forward. More worrying, however, are the messages at the heart of her fascination with cultural violence. 'Repression makes meaning and purpose' she says. It is the kind of slogan that could have decorated the gates of Auschwitz, alongside *Arbeit Macht Frei*.

HEARTY APPETITES

Edmund White (ed), *The Faber Book of Gay Short Fiction*
(London: Faber, 1991)

There is no longer anything particularly new about anthologies
of gay fiction. For over a decade British and American publishing
houses have been meeting gay men's apparently voracious
demand for short stories about themselves. The two most
comprehensive anthologies to date were both American: Stephen
Wright's *Different* (1974) and Seymour Kleinberg's *The Other
Persuasion* (1977). Most other collections have been of stories by
contemporary writers only.

Wright's book, a low-cost paperback, was a rather capricious
mixture of elements. Of twenty-four stories, two were by women,
one was a translation from the French, two were excerpted from
novels, four were by one author ('Phil Andros'). The stories
spanned the period from 1894 to 1974, but appeared in random
order. Kleinberg's collection from much the same period, 1893
to 1975, was arranged chronologically, and had a slightly better
balanced gender mix: nine women writers to seventeen men. The
stories were presented under three historical subdivisions:
'Underground', 'On the Fringe: From Tragedy to Camp' and
'Inside: Toward New Definitions'. This doctrinaire structure,
insisting on progress as well as progression, was misleadingly
definitive.

In the new Faber anthology, Edmund White has taken a
more relaxed approach to the same course of development.
Although he has excluded lesbian writers and based his
subsequent choice on a peculiarly narrow view of who gay men
are (he says 'most gays are urban'), he has succeeded in gathering
a richly varied range of voices.

In a rather loosely written foreword, White argues that 'being
gay is a bit like being a writer'. Every gay man's coming out,
whether to himself or to others, soon becomes a polished and
much repeated narrative, in relation to which he is both detached
and most closely involved. The man who comes out is, like the
gay writer, 'forging an identity as much as revealing it'. In
addition, gay fiction has carried a double burden of 'the obligation
to explain and the ambition to excite'. What White does not
mention is that this means gay writers are serving two quite

distinct audiences, divided by sexual orientation itself. An implicit friction between these two groups is what produces the sharpest ironies of Camp.

In reference to the current development of Lesbian and Gay Studies in American academic institutions, White says: 'The 1990s may be the decade when gay fiction will be institutionalized'. It is to be hoped that he has noticed the joke. Gay identity has only recently emerged from fear of the madhouse; it is too soon to go back. But what one does notice in the present collection is a mad hilarity beneath the grave business of self-identification. Men who have been treated as jokes are taking themselves seriously, yet at the same time rocking with pre-emptive laughter.

The policy of including extracts from novels is not always satisfactory. Strictly, a short fragment of a long work of fiction is not 'short fiction'. James Purdy is usually better at greater length, and James Baldwin's piece, an extract from the undervalued novel *Just Above My Head* (1979), seems flabby out of its cumulative context. On the other hand, a piece by Alan Hollinghurst is all the more powerful for having been released from the lumbering plot of *The Swimming-Pool Library*. A chapter of William Burroughs' *The Wild Boys* also works well on its own and reminds us that, contrary to those critics who see him only as a foul-mouthed pornographer, Burroughs can be the most meticulous of stylists, with a highly lyrical imagination.

The collection's most obvious omission is James Stern's 'Travellers' Tears' (1938), an extraordinarily positive story for its time, both light-hearted and sentimentally profound, with much to say about both sexes and, unusually, a wide range of ages. Lonnie Coleman's 'The Theban Warriors' (1955) would also have looked good here. Tennessee Williams might have been better represented by one of his wierder tales ('One Arm', for instance) instead of 'Two on a Party' which is, by his standards, rather dull. An Angus Wilson would not have gone amiss; 'Et Dona Ferentes' is the obvious choice. But, in truth, there is so much good writing here that to complain about omissions of one's favourites becomes an exercise in vanity.

As for the arrangement, it looks, at first, as though White intends to chart gay history with sicknesses. The early stories, representing the newly defined and pathologised consciousness of 'the homosexual', all concern men or boys who are ailing. They all combine dicky hearts with hearty appetites. The reader waits

to see which will consume the other first; usually it is the heart
that succumbs. Henry James' 'The Pupil' exercises the Master's
ponderous wit in a slow crescendo to a splendidly silly climax,
where the prospect of fulfilled love causes a pursued boy's heart
to burst. (In some ways the story is a rationalist dry-run for 'The
Turn of the Screw', but much less purposefully poised.) In the
final chapter of Ronald Firbank's *Cardinal Pirelli*, which comes
next, it is the pursuer who expires of excitement. E.M. Forster's
'Dr Woolacott' reaches a similar loving climax in death.

   Sickliness is active in Denton Welch's strainingly hearty
'When I Was Thirteen'; bowel cancer in the Alfred Chester;
hepatitis and a fatally 'malformed heart' in the Gore Vidal. One
begins to worry that, having begun thus, the book will end with
the AIDS crisis and, therefore, leave an impression less of the
nuptial couch than of the hospital bed. But White has made a
strategic decision to place the AIDS-related stories — by himself,
Andrew Holleran, Armistead Maupin and Adam Mars-Jones —
in the heart of the book, and to follow them with work on other
topics by younger writers. The intention is presumably to
emphasise that there is, as it were, life after AIDS.

   One strong thread of continuity connecting different stages
in modern gay history is a sense of displacement. Gay youths do
not fit into macho schoolboy gangs; gay couples are conspicuous
on suburban avenues. Where do we belong? It is as well, then,
that the first of the authors included here is the laureate of
dislocation, Henry James. His story, and those by Gore Vidal,
David Plante and Edmund White himself, are about Americans
in Europe. Denton Welch, Christopher Isherwood and Simon
Burt look at the British in Europe. The fact is, of course, that
many gay men have to leave home, or even the home culture,
before they can come out. Before spending everything on travel,
they would do well to heed one of the characters in Patrick Gale's
exquisite story 'The List': 'Abroad doesn't count as long as your
mother has a room full of your things'.

   It is a measure of the strength of the later writers, that both
Henry James and Ronald Firbank come off badly by comparison.
This is a salutory lesson for the kinds of literary critic who
continue to insist that gay liberation has ruined the literature
of homosexuality by forcing it out of the closet of metaphor. In
fact, the very explicit stories with which this book ends are no
less ingenious, in terms of literary trope, than the more sexually
oblique work with which it begins.

One of the most striking things about gay men's recent erotic writing — in this book as elsewhere — is the degree to which the kinds of passage homophobic critics like to dismiss as mere pornographic description actually offer metaphysical transformations of physical events. For all the futurity that heterosexual writers evoke in their descriptions of reproductive intercourse, few hetero-erotic texts can compete with their gay counterparts for sheer weight of significance.

Indeed, there are times when one could do with less meaning. Reading from cover to cover, one hits a patch about two-thirds of the way through the book when a surfeit of highly sophisticated formulations of desire makes one long for some simple, old-fashioned ignorance. All these sensitive, intellectual narrators can become as tiresome as their lovers' invariably hard-toned washboard stomachs. Moreover, this middle generation of writers seems to find money, as much as male flesh, not only desirable but sexy. So it is a relief to encounter Timothy Ireland's story about men on ordinary incomes, and Neil Bartlett's characteristic piece about poor men living as though they were filthy rich. Like so many of the best gay characters since Wilde or Genet, they dine out on dreams.

To return to the point about increasing explicitness: no censored book is as good as it might have been. It follows that the literature of 'homosexuality', since the invention of the word in 1869 and its entry into the English language in 1892, has been marred by heterosexual interference. The whole point of the recent gay writing since 1969 has been the understanding that it will eventually, inevitably, excel itself. Only give it time. But it will do so as *homosexual literature*, not as a heterosexual-sanctioned, muffled and gagged literature of the unspeakable. It may be, therefore, that heterosexual readers will never fully recognise and appreciate the extent of its improvement. The gay writer must make his own choice about whether this matters.

This is a monumental book: large, of course, but also seriously representative. White has taken an expansive body of work and licked it into shape. It emerges strong and sleek, dangerously competitive. And like any efficient physique, it is also beautiful.

DELICACY AND DARING

Christopher Bram, *Surprising Myself* (London: GMP, 1989)

Joel Scherzenlieb, the narrator and central character of this novel, has good reason to be continually surprised by himself. His rite of passage from unconfident adolescence to unconfident adulthood is packed with the implausibilities of real life.

Against a muted political background (Vietnam, Watergate) and some of gay American fiction's commonest characters (the villainous straight brother-in-law, the understanding boyfriend who has minored in philosophy), Christopher Bram depicts the familiar but confusing territory where gay and straight worlds overlap. Yet the subject's familiarity is never a problem: for Bram is not content to do familiar things with it.

He has taken a relatively narrow field, comprising hardly more than six characters from a single family, and has allowed himself ample space in which to develop them in detail, yet never so intensely as to lose his lightness of touch. The result is a comedy both moving and, at times, profound.

The author is as good at the withholding of information as he is at telling us what we need to know. Better still, he knows how to change gear with an effortless fluency. This enables him to achieve an unforced transition between stretches of static introspection and others of fast-paced plot. At least one chapter is as breathtaking as a rollercoaster ride.

Virtually every page has a detail worth applauding, from the unobtrusive moment when a character shouts the word 'whimper' at the top of his voice, to a description of a laboriously considerate fuck: 'It was a slow process, full of commands and requests, as if we were parking a truck.'

To read a long gay novel (424 pages) is a pleasure in itself. But to find one whose quality matches up to its size and is sustained more or less consistently throughout, is really rare.

Christopher Bram, *Hold Tight* (London: GMP, 1990)

When sailor Hank Fayette gets caught in a male brothel in New York shortly after Pearl Harbor, the US Navy makes him an offer he can't refuse. If he wants to escape punishment, he will have to accept being set up in the brothel as bait to catch Nazi spies. Since Hank enjoys sex, he embraces his whoredom with a hard-on and good cheer.

What follows is a thriller in which the reader always knows more than the characters about what is really going on. This gives the book both its relaxed suspense and its humour. In virtually every scene, somebody is misunderstanding someone else, and the reader is in on the joke. There are enough crossed purposes here to service a farce, but it is a measure of the author's skill that the book is never farcical. Bram keeps the reader ahead of the characters, yet is himself always several paces ahead of all of us. He keeps us in a constant state of both knowing and guessing at once.

The manners and customs of the brothel are meticulously 'observed' (by which I mean invented). Bram's descriptions, though brief and always geared to the furtherance of the plot, can be both funny and devastatingly accurate — as in this tiny sketch of machismo in action: 'He walked with his legs far apart, as if he had to step around his genitals.'

The book's sexual politics are up to date, yet Bram succeeds in applying them carefully to the 1940s in a way that is neither anachronistic nor laboured — a genuinely difficult balancing act to pull off. He also manages to write about sex as if he finds it thrilling. It therefore fits well into the fabric of the thriller.

It seems that Bram will prove, eventually, more uncompromising than David Leavitt, even if he has a little less than Leavitt's measure of technical gloss. The thing I most admire about Bram is his willingness to take risks, not only by trying a new fictional genre, but by plunging into thorny issues, like race, with a rare combination of delicacy and daring. This is a gay writer with ambition.

Christopher Bram, *In Memory of Angel Clare* (London: GMP, 1991)

When filmmaker Clarence Laird dies at 38, his friends close ranks around Michael, his 23 year-old lover, for a decent period of mourning. But Michael is young and embittered, and his egotism offends theirs. One by one, the older friends grow tired of him.

Arguments erupt about who was best at looking after Clarence when he was ill, and who has mourned him most since his death. Eventually, the two lesbian friends who have acquired

Clarence's apartment tell Michael he must move out. No one sees the real depth of his depression. They think he is just crying wolf.

What results is a subtle, if somewhat hurried, account of the development of genuine friendships. Unlike Bram's first two novels, this one does not have a tightly structured plot. It relies on the single developing situation to retain our interest and sympathy. If, at times, it risks losing both, it does so because of the seriousness of its aims.

The book is at its worst when a ponderous, didactic tone creeps in. If this appears in conspicuous places it is hard to tolerate — as when a chapter starts with the sentence 'Memory is imperfect knowledge'. This is both banal and unclear, and does nothing to tell or enrich the tale. The problem seems to be that, approaching the subject of AIDS and its consequences, Bram has slightly lost his nerve.

He does, however, display his usual lightness of touch with descriptive detail, even when describing more than mere visual detail. He barely needs to add anything to one devastating sentence about Michael in the fifth chapter: 'His springy hair curled around his ears like hurt feelings'. The whole of the character is there.

Bram does not, for the most part, deal in stereotypes. Even minor characters come across as plausible individuals. I was pleased to read in a gay novel, for a change, the description of Clarence's brother as 'a Fundamentalist but a decent man'. The word 'but' says enough, politically, for Bram not to have to make this man a villain.

PROBLEM PAGE

Ray Hamble, *What's Wrong With My Willy?* (London: GMP, 1991)

Dear Dr. Woods,
What's wrong with *What's Wrong With My Willy?*
Yours, R.H.

Dear R.H.,
I've thought about your problem for some days, and I'm
forced to the conclusion that you are a victim of poor advice.
Whoever told you you were capable of writing a useful book was
either ignorant of what such a task should involve, or was having
a laugh at your expense. In either case, I have a great deal of
sympathy for your unfortunate plight.
Let's begin with your attitudes to a number of issues which
centrally concern the lives of gay men in this country. You
subscribe to the homophobic view that for many gay men —
namely, the ones who write to you about their sexual and
emotional problems — 'gayness is the greatest of all misnomers'.
The problem here is that you have confused 'gayness' with the
minutiae of dysfunction, in a manner which, since it appears on
the second page of your introduction, seems to invite the reader
to interpret all that follows as a catalogue of the ills of gayness
itself, rather than of slighter human failings and foibles regardless
of sexual orientation. Homosexuality does not necessitate
unhappiness, and you should not appear to let any of your
correspondents and readers go on believing in such myths.
Similarly, further down the same introductory page, you
state that 'the world of gay sex is an odd one'. Odd to whom?
And is it really any odder than the world of straight sex? If a
gay sexual counsellor holds and publicly expresses such views,
how shall we ever persuade young gay people to stop thinking
of themselves as abnormal?
Some of your reasoning is very weak indeed. For instance:
'I'd prefer not to have a "political" voice in the gay community.
That would mean taking sides and my whole aim is to remain
neutral.' Does this really mean that, on the vital health issues
with which you claim to be concerned, you are totally unwilling
to take any stand against the murderous indifference and

complacency of those who do not particularly care whether we live or die? If a man in your influential position rejects the option of a political stance in favour of the gay community, he is *ipso facto* taking sides against gay people by default.

You account for the fact that you are still, at the age of 58, leading a closeted double life ('Ray Hamble' is a pseudonym) by telling us that you are a Gemini and, bloody-mindedly, that you 'have no intention of changing'. This, of course, is your own business. Or rather, it would have been if you had not mentioned it in your introduction. I wonder how you imagine you are in a position to counsel new generations of gay men to whom even the Stonewall Riot is ancient history. I am thinking, in particular, of the teenager whom you tell that 16 is too early for a boy to come out.

For an 'expert' on the matters you write about, you are astonishingly vague or ill-informed. I soon stopped noting down the occasions when, faced with a heartfelt request for information, you reply with phrases like 'your guess is as good as mine', or 'I'm sure I don't know why but I guess that your analysis is as good as any'. On the difficult subject of child abuse, you write: 'I may hold one view. Someone else may hold another. Who is to say who is right and who is wrong?' On some topics (say, the flavours of ice creams), these remarks would, simply, be so unhelpfully self-evident that they would have been better left unsaid; but on child abuse they are culpably stupid.

You frequently abdicate the responsibility to offer real advice. I must admit to having cackled like the Wicked Witch when you replied to one correspondent: 'Your analysis of the situation is probably quite good: it sounds quite professional anyway.' What a pity that the same cannot be said for your own analyses. Very often, you are reduced to summing up the world in the most blitheringly banal ways: 'We all have our funny little ways,' for instance. Are people seriously expected to pay for this?

You show a certain interest in the history of sexuality. I was fascinated by your analysis of the origins of fetishism: 'Fetishism to do with clothing goes back to the beginning of time with the skins of animals providing man's first form of attire. There is, therefore, something very primitive in the love of leather.' I seem to have missed a step in the logic of this argument; but your conclusion is, doubtless, correct. It was all the more surprising, then, when you ascribed recent origins to a whole raft of sexual acts and aids. Let me mention only your claim that, in 1952, dildoes were 'still waiting to be invented'. Tell that to the Whore of Babylon.

At times your analysis of health matters is vague to the extent of being dangerous. For example, when speaking of the risk of contracting HIV by sucking cocks, you conclude: 'If there is a risk it must be very remote indeed, and even more remote for the guy who is having his cock gobbled on. I think, however, that anyone would be tempting fate just a little too complacently if he were to "suck and be damned" with someone he knew to be HIV-positive.' This shows that you have misunderstood the crucial point about Safer Sex — without which it is nothing but a pious phrase — namely, that *every* gay man should be performing *every* sexual act in *every* sexual relationship as if he and his partner(s) knew they were HIV+. Anything less is madness.

A word in your shell-like about your sense of humour. While I agree that such a book as yours ought not to be heavily solemn, I did find the sheer mass of (oft repeated) doubles entendres, together with signal exclamation marks, unfunny. They betray an almost pathological embarrassment behind the equanimity which they are apparently intended to mimic. While talking about the possibility that a man might get a hard-on in a nudist camp, you end a sentence as follows: 'the problem just doesn't arise (oops! pardon the pun)'. This is not an isolated case. I blush for you.

Finally, since neither you nor your editors have taken the trouble to compose an index of the 'problems' covered, any reader who wants an urgent response to a particular issue will have to wade through the whole book, and run the risk of not finding what he is looking for. I would advise him to look elsewhere. There is, within the pages of your book, a lot of sensible advice — especially of the type which calls on a reader to worry less about a minor scare. I am willing to concede that many men will have had their fears allayed, over the years, by reading your columns in gay magazines; and I accept that you have devoted a lot of energy to replying personally to individual correspondents. What a terrible pity, then, that you have undermined your admirable intentions, here, with such shoddy execution.

DEATH OF THE AUTHOR

Pier Vittorio Tondelli, *Separate Rooms* (London: Serpent's Tail, 1992)

Increasingly, as the calamity of our era develops and takes its toll, works of art representing AIDS, by artists who actually had AIDS, are being packaged as being, not only particularly authentic, but also able to convey a particularly vivid *frisson* of sadness. Publishers and distributors are alert to the commercial potential of real 'tragedy'. One has heard of the theoretical 'death of the author', but in actuality death sells.

When the film *Les Nuits Fauves (Savage Nights)* recently opened in this country, every preview and review referred to the fact that the director Cyril Collard had 'died of AIDS' just a few days before the film received a fist-full of awards at the Cannes film festival. This meaningless coincidence was invariably claimed as giving the film added 'poignancy'. Without the affirming imprimatur of Collard's death, it would have been just another film about AIDS.

Separate Rooms, too, is a case in point. On the back cover James Kirkup is quoted as saying, 'Its heartbreak and tragedy are realities, for Tondelli died of AIDS on 16th December, 1991, at the age of 36.' The implication of this statement is that, had Tondelli not 'died of AIDS', the sadness of the book would have been, not a 'reality', but mere fiction. Kirkup's covert value judgement refers not only to the validating presence of AIDS in the purest of its manifestations — that is, in the 'reality' which kills — but also to the comparative insignificance of purely imaginative fiction.

To my mind, regardless of the author's life, regardless even of his death, the 'heartbreak and tragedy' of a book about AIDS derive from many deaths, past and to come. A novel about AIDS may be fiction, but its subject is, inevitably, a social reality. AIDS is not a fantasy. Refuse to identify with it if you dare.

Separate Rooms is the story of an affair conducted between two men at a respectful distance, in the metaphorical 'separate rooms' of the title. Separated, too, by nationality, culture and first language — Leo is Italian, Thomas German — the two lovers live up to a very contemporary vision of European togetherness and, on occasions when the vision falters, apartness.

The book belongs to a genre of gay male nomadism which, at a stretch, could be traced back to Victorian men's accounts of their erotic wanderings in Sir Richard Burton's 'Sotadic zone'. Be that as it may, post-Stonewall fiction offers countless examples of the gay travelogue, which constitutes either a journey from body to body across a fairly limited geographical space (as in John Rechy's *Numbers* or Renaud Camus's *Tricks*) or a literal tour of widespread locations in which such bodies might be encountered (as in Aldo Busi's *Sodomies in Eleven Point*). Either way, the Grand Tour is one way of representing what some people call 'promiscuity' — namely the unremarkable, cumulative sex lives which many gay men share. Such men are tourists in the flesh, speeding on a whistle-stop trip, not from capital to capital, but from man to man.

In this case, however, the protagonists are involved in a more or less monogamous relationship. Travel is not the sign and instrument of sexual restlessness, but a way of relating meaningfully to the world and to each other. As in an American road movie, the very condition of being on the move serves to validate what would otherwise appear to be an eventless — which is to say, a purposeless — existence. Furthermore, since the relationship itself is international, travel is a way of experiencing both its weakness and its strength.

Tondelli makes many of his points about the effects which illness and love have on each other through juxtapositions of contrasting physical states. For instance, a lushly explicit account of Leo and Thomas's first night together is immediately followed by a hospital scene, with an emaciated Thomas immobilised among catheters and drip feeds. Similarly, later on, Tondelli alternates scenes of sex and surgery. This ploy may well be unsubtle — it is certainly not particularly original — but it is very effective.

True to a convention which was established very early in the epidemic, the word AIDS is not mentioned once in the novel. One presumes that most writers intend this tactic to give their books a sense of universality: the illness could be any illness, the deaths any deaths. This is humbug. No book ever gained much by being imprecise. Even though it is widespread, AIDS is no more a part of the 'human condition' than gayness itself is not worth mentioning because it is identical to all other human sexualities. Social reality tells us otherwise. The unwillingness to name either the sexuality or the syndrome is a habit learnt in the closet.

A JOLLY MARTYRDOM

Derek Jarman, *At Your Own Risk: A Saint's Testament* (London: Hutchinson, 1992)

On 22 September 1991, at a ceremonial laying-on of hands by the Sisters of Perpetual Indulgence, Derek Jarman was officially declared a saint. Hence the subtitle of his latest book. The great advantage of being canonized while you are still living is that you do not have to rely on others to keep the record of your virtues.

Jarman has been polishing his talents as an auto-hagiographer ever since the publication of *Dancing Ledge* in 1984. *Modern Nature* was the most coherent and moving of the written texts — a diary of gardening, filming and coping with HIV. While similarly rooted in its author's daily life, and similarly a testament to his rage and courage, *At Your Own Risk* goes beyond autobiography into the politics of sexuality and health care.

A chronological scrapbook, it surveys the life of a man who grew up as a queer in the fifties and sixties, became gay in the early seventies, and has recently been transformed into a queer again. (One should note, though, that there is a world of difference between a pre-gay queer and a post-gay queer.) He has also come out for a second time, this time as having HIV. The story is familiar from many interviews, but somehow survives frequent retelling.

Trained as a painter, Jarman has tended to build up his films — even the adaptations of classic texts — around visual ideas rather than scripts. This is what makes his version of *The Tempest*, despite its tiny budget, the most magical of all *Tempests*. Paradoxically, on the other hand, there are times when his *Caravaggio* becomes too turgidly verbal for its subject. Similarly, his books are at their best when not going out of their way to be poetic. When he is not at pains to make them seem beautiful, his descriptions of his garden at Dungeness are beautiful indeed. By the same criterion, his best accounts of sexual encounters are the most off-hand and down-to-earth.

Though no master of literary form, Jarman seems at ease with the haphazard inclusiveness of journals and scrapbooks. Juxtaposition is, of course, a filmic strategy. It was adopted by the mandarins of literary modernism only after they had seen it at work in popular movies. Furthermore, like many gay artists influenced by the art of the paradox, Jarman is a practised hand at oxymoron. One thinks of the most striking juxtapositions in his films: Elisabeth Welch singing 'Stormy Weather' in *The Tempest*, the anachronisms in *Caravaggio*, Annie Lennox singing 'Every Time We Say Goodbye' in *Edward II*.

One of the other most consistent tendencies in Jarman's career has been his identification of, and with, a long succession of homosexual artists and their artistry. 'An orgasm joins you to the past,' he says, which may come as a surprise to readers more familiar with heterosexual intercourse's claims on futurity. Having enormous respect for his sexual forefathers, he has been profoundly influenced by Sergei Eisenstein and Pier Paolo Pasolini. In his work on the gay 'tradition', he has identified with Caravaggio and Christopher Marlowe, used a selection of Shakespeare's sonnets as a screenplay, set to film Benjamin Britten's setting-to-music of Wilfred Owen's poems, and so forth. It was therefore with understandable exasperation that Jarman commented, in *Modern Nature*, 'what more traditional subject matter could a film-maker take on? And yet I'm still seen by some as a menace.'

Menace or not, he does take it as one of his saintly duties to disturb — some might say, to cause offence. His justification might be that he, too, has been mightily offended. This book's climax consists of a harrowing sequence of recent press cuttings about homosexuality and the HIV crisis. Here, Jarman has alternated fatuous tabloid headlines ('PULPIT POOFS CAN STAY', 'LESBIAN TEACHER HORROR') with the more temperate voices of the gay press. This short anthology of threatened lives and offensive rhetoric is, on its own, enough to account for the unmeasured anger of the rest of the book.

As one can tell from his long-running dispute with Sir Ian McKellen over whether one should feast with panthers or take tea with prime ministers, Jarman is in no mood for conciliation. As saintly testaments go, *At Your Own Risk* is a relatively splenetic text. There are no miracles here, but one's breath is taken, and taken often, by Jarman's visions of a nation corrupted by its own press. His premature and distinctly jolly martyrdom seems focused, purposeful and full of faith.

NOTES ON QUEER

(1992)

1 Queer culture must be explicit. The post-gay queer is out of the closet.
2 Queer culture is defined and shaped only by queers. Queer is a name we call ourselves; we must question the motives of non-queers who call us by it.
3 Queer culture must not compromise with straight values.
4 Queer culture does not give a damn about equality with straight people; at the same time, it demands literal equality in all points of law.
5 Queer culture seeks not to fit in but to stand out.
6 Queer culture does not aim to be understood by its enemies; self-justification belongs to the past.
7 Queer culture wastes no time in projecting 'positive' images; it reclaims and takes pride in negative images. 'One of the problems was that with the word "gay" came a drive for positive images, but all the artists I knew and respected were involved with negative images because that was the intelligent thing to do in a culture which promoted all that false positivity through advertising and so on. What was positive? White, middle class, male? I don't know. No one ever defined it.' (Derek Jarman)
8 Queer culture must recognise that there are male queers and female queers, and that neither group can flourish without the other.
9 Queer culture must welcome diversity and distrust uniformity.
10 Queer culture is an urban culture, and must recognise its limitations as such. 'If you are struggling to be Gay in rural Britain, the last thing you want is someone more fortunate telling you that you don't measure up because you can't think of yourself as Queer.' (Alan Sinfield)
11 Queer culture must cohere around a sense of community; there should be no such thing as an isolated queer.
12 Queer culture is an international culture, but must recognise the limitations of the fact that its values spring from those of the developed 'West'.
13 Queer culture must involve itself in health education. 'The

Aids epidemic hit gay men, and brought home the message that we are still queers in the eyes of society.' (Keith Alcorn)

14 The highest aim of any queer cultural text or event should be to save lives. The lives we fail to save we must commemorate.

15 Queer culture is not a novelty. It must recognise the debt it owes to previous gay cultures; in particular, it has inherited the structures and stratagems of Camp.

16 Queer culture is not a licence to harass lesbians and gay men. It does not replace lesbian and gay cultures; it supplements them.

17 Queer culture is not a fashion accessory; but it will, of course, develop its own fashions.

18 Queer culture is not a political fashion accessory; being queer is not, in itself, a free ticket to radical sainthood.

19 Queer culture exists in the real world, and exists only to engage with reality; queer is not an idle dream.

20 Queer culture is a sexual culture, even if individual queers are celibate. For us, sexual events are cultural events. Pornography holds a very special place among our strategies for representing ourselves to each other.

21 Queer culture worships the body, but is not fooled by it.

22 Queer culture must question the politics and ethics of 'beauty'.

23 Queer culture is concerned with depths as well as surfaces.

24 Queer culture is playful but not frivolous, and serious but not solemn.

25 Queer culture is low culture and high culture, having rejected distinctions between the two.

26 Queer culture rejects systems and orthodoxies.

27 Queer culture is atheistic.

28 Queer culture and queer politics are one and the same; queer culture is a political culture.

SMOKED SAUSAGE

Hubert Fichte, *The Orphanage* and *Detlev's Imitations* (London: Serpent's Tail, 1990 and 1993)

The Orphanage is a novel about the life of a small boy in Nazi Germany. Although his mother is alive and can visit him, Detlev is effectively an orphan. He lives in a Catholic orphanage where everything is organised to deny him the existence of his father, a Jew. With such a parent there can literally be no future for the boy. So life demands denials as much as breath.

Fichte captures the menace of Detlev's life in close detail. The best thing about the book is the way it shows how Nazism, Catholicism and the ordinary terrorism of childhood games all merge seamlessly. Detlev would be bullied under any regime.

The second volume of the trilogy, *Detlev's Imitations,* inevitably fills out Detlev's character. Not only does it depict the first stirrings of a homosexual puberty in the months after the fire-bombing of Hamburg in 1943, but it starts looking back at the boy from the viewpoint of the adult he has become by 1968. As a result, the adult reader has a more solid sense of purchase on Detlev's mind, and, indeed, on the eccentricities of Fichte's narrative method.

Fichte weaves impressive connections between the history which led to the bombing of Hamburg and the history of the oppression of gay men by the Nazis. However, he makes it uncomfortably clear that such things do not work simply: if the war was run by villains, there were villains on both sides.

So retribution rains down on Hamburg's gay scene, not from the Nazis but from the Allies: Bomber Harris is to Hamburg as 'God' was to Sodom. The bombing occurred on 17 May (17/5), a date which Detlev later associates with paragraph 175, the Nazis' main instrument for the control of homosexuality.

If one night's cathartic fire-storm had anything to do with liberation, the freedom it burned into the dying Reich did not extend to perverts. The Allies did not repeal paragraph 175. And the law's eventual abolition, decades later, led, as in England and Wales, to an increase in arrests.

The clearest early sign of Detlev's gayness comes in his reaction to the soldiers of the occupying army. He gazes in awe at the drum-tight backsides of their uniforms: 'More than anything else Detlev would like to crawl between the halves of the English arse. He imagines that in there it must smell of smoked sausage.'

This dream of refuge in a liberating soldier's arse is not isolated, of course. While it does constitute the start of the boy's erotic life, it also foreshadows the politics of his adult life. At one later point he says, 'If I'm honest, I can only conceive of freedom as a gigantic worldwide homosexualisation'. This mistrust of democracy's heterosexual institutions is similar to feminist scepticism. It questions the whole self-celebrating structure of the 'West'.

As notes towards the definition of 'liberation' and 'liberty' as they might apply to gay men (rather than to men like the philandering pseudo-Berliner John F. Kennedy), Fichte's sequence of novels becomes increasingly complex and sophisticated, if not particularly moving. It seems to be leading to depressing conclusions. To creep into the warmth of a soldier's protection may provide temporary relief (not to mention smoked sausage). But does such forced confinement have much to do with freedom?

INDISCRIMINATE TENDERNESS

Paul Bailey, *Sugar Cane* (London: Bloomsbury, 1993)

When Paul Bailey's novel *Gabriel's Lament* was first published
and subsequently shortlisted for the 1986 Booker Prize, it became
a common critical strategy to attempt to locate Bailey's work in
the Great Tradition by comparing him with Dickens. A reviewer
in the *Guardian* even used the oddly Dickensian adverb
'Dickensianly'. This is not necessarily as great a compliment as
it may sound. Often, by contemporary critical standards, a novel
will merit the comparison if it is merely set in a city — preferably
London — and peopled with eccentrics. By these criteria, *Gabriel's
Lament* was Dickensian indeed. But what Bailey seems to lack
in the Dickens department is a clear sense of social purpose and
a focussed interest in reaching a popular audience. Despite the
rather earthy topics he confronts, his voice is fastidious,
expressing a consistently refined sensibility. The truth is, he is
too subtle to be truly Dickensian.

His new novel is connected with *Gabriel's Lament* (such links
have become a habit of his) by adopting as its narrator the
venereologist, Dr Esther Potocki, with whom Gabriel Harvey
formed a relationship at the end of the earlier novel. When an
AIDS patient in her hospital dies, one of his ex-lovers turns his
attention to Esther and, for reasons which are not clear to her,
befriends her. This young man turns out to be secretive and
enigmatic. We soon learn that the name by which Esther knows
him, Stephen, is an alias; he has many other names for many
other occasions. It is only after a long period of confidence-building
that he feels able to confirm Esther's suspicions about how he
makes his living: he rents out his body to the needy. But it is
not only he who performs a protracted dance of more than seven
veils. The narrative, too, tends to withhold information which
Stephen himself could hardly have concealed if he had wanted
to. It is only by the way, for instance, that we learn he is black.

Although the book raises 'social issues', it also fights shy of
them. Bailey has far more interest in character than in argument
or plot. Once he raises a topical concern, he seems unsure of
what to do with it. Disbelief needs the kind of suspension only
the likes of Judge Jeffries could offer before one can comfortably
accept a venereologist narrator, and a Londoner at that, who

never uses the word AIDS. (She coyly refers to 'the awful acronym'.) This is an indication of the extent to which Bailey skirts round the realities of the London he purports to describe.

The consequent lightness of tone is not, though, a trivialising force. Its avoidances generate tension around areas of the unspoken, almost as if they were truly unspeakable. Sociology evaporates into evasive tittle-tattle with a nervous edge. We have heard this kind of tone before. Its two mid-century masters were Patrick White and Angus Wilson, in whose novels an unrestrained voice of ironic and ironised gossip was given such free rein that it often approached the point of self-parody. It was at this point that their novels were most vulnerable to attack from heterosexually-identified critics, but connoisseurs of camp judged them sublime if not divine.

Like Wilson, Bailey is adept at fluent chatter. *Gabriel's Lament* offered a hubbub of articulate voices, all unwittingly competing to make the most bizarre utterances seem like common sense. Even if some of them sounded so similar as to become virtually indistinguishable from each other, the novel's achievement was to make this babble sound neither implausible nor particularly unusual. It persuaded one, temporarily, that everyone speaks like that.

Where this facility of Bailey's can create a problem is in the representation of less articulate people. Stephen, who starts out as such a character, somehow turns into a vividly persuasive speaker by the time he is expected to take over from Esther the duty of narrating. Bailey seems to regard this as a question of will rather than ability. He has enough of a novelist's optimism to believe that anyone who wishes to speak fluently will find the ability to do so. This small miracle may require some readers to stretch their credulity, but it is fully in keeping with Bailey's broader moral vision of a social world of limitless possibilities.

Moral vision is, of course, one of the qualities for which we in this country like to congratulate our novelists; and Bailey does indeed deliver in this respect. His fiction constitutes an eloquent plea for the eradication of all the 'isms' whose names you would never catch him using: ageism, racism, sexism, heterosexism and so forth. But it is a curiously indeterminate and muted moral vision which sees liberals as saints, and devils as misled unfortunates. The problem is that even the villainous characters here are not villains. Bailey treats all of his characters with indiscriminate tenderness. To that extent, he is more Dickens than Dostoyevsky. This is the kind of liberalism which would rather hold a convict's hand than chop it off — admirable in real life, but in fiction potentially a bit of a bore.

Stephen's involvement with a bogus bishop who runs a male brothel (based on true events, the publisher feels the need to claim) provides some ribald entertainment, even though the promise of sexual revelations is never really kept. A less than candid Candide, Stephen narrates his own life with stoic understatement, leaving the impression that many troubles and indignities remain untold. Esther is far more forthcoming; her relationship with her mother is classic Paul Bailey, beautifully unfolded.

While recognising that Bailey's fiction is not meant to be dramatically plotted, even so one must inevitably find the ending of *Sugar Cane* anti-climactic. The main character simply vanishes. If the fact that the narrator names her newly-born son after him (or one of his manifestations) is meant in some way to compensate for this, and provide a symbolic continuity, it fails to do so. All it means is that there are now two Stephens, two uncertain futures, at large. However, it may be churlish to complain when a novelist leaves the unresolvable unresolved. Stephen was always too inscrutable to marry or to die.

WHY POETRY?

John Harold (ed), *How Can You Write a Poem When You're Dying of AIDS?* (London: Cassell, 1993)

This book is packed with clichés about love and death. Lovers are 'intoxicated' by each other's eyes, or 'lost' in each other's beauty. Hearts are 'thirsty'. The dead reappear in the sky as stars. Death is compared with the metamorphosis of a caterpillar into a butterfly. Only rarely and unexpectedly does a fresh metaphor cut through the staleness of the assembled poets' responses to AIDS. Readers who come to poetry for linguistic precision and clarity of emotional focus will be severely disappointed that an anthology on the epidemic could contain so much sloppy writing.

Worse still, these borrowed ideas are often expressed in 'poetic' language — which is to say, fragments of the kind of language which good poets used in the nineteenth century and before — in some forlorn (and unnecessary) attempt to give serious literary weight to mere human emotions. So the morning becomes 'morn'. Both sea and sky appear in the plural form which TV news journalists also resort to when confronted by human tragedy: 'seas', 'skies'. Object and verb are inverted. How such archaic devices are expected to cope with the most definitively post-modern of epidemics is not clear.

On the other hand, it may be that we should give clichés the benefit of their cultural value. Clearly, people use and re-use them not only because they can't think of anything better, but because these are the most readily available, and the most easily recognisable, phrases in our cultural store.

Most of the familiar noises in this book are not just random echoes from the market-place of British life. They can be traced back directly to, and to precise moments in, the tradition of the English elegy. For instance, the trope in which the dead lover is immortalized as a star in the night sky can be followed back, through Walt Whitman's 'When lilacs last in the dooryard bloom'd', to Percy Shelley's 'Adonaïs' and beyond. When we want to write in commemoration of dead friends and lovers, we turn to these canonical precedents. The dominant culture's other main sources for grieving are Christian scriptures and hymnals.

But why poetry? Surely we all agree that poetry is elitist,

apolitical drivel which, thank goodness, doesn't sell. So what is
the motivation behind such projects? I know of at least two other
AIDS-related poetry anthologies currently being prepared in this
country. Michael Klein's impressive *Poets for Life* (USA, 1989)
set the standard to which these must aspire.

The fact is that it is as much *popular* culture as high culture
which resorts to verse when reacting to deaths. Poetry's
usefulness in expressing grief has by no means expired even in
our prosaic times. Any day of the week, the personal columns of
your local newspaper will contain In Memoriam ads in tortured
rhyming couplets. Here is an example I picked up this afternoon:
'To have you for my Mother was cause enough for pride, no-one
could ever equal you, no matter how they tried. I lost a Mother
in a million, I loved you to the end, I lost two special things that
day, my Mother and my friend. You were a Mother with a heart
of gold, how much I miss you can never be told. You shared my
troubles and helped me along, so if I follow your footsteps I'll
never go wrong. You were a Mother so very rare, always willing,
always there. You left behind one aching heart that loved you
most sincere. I never shall and never will forget you Mother dear.
God bless you always--your broken-hearted son.'

It is the very clumsiness of this attempt to rise to the level
of greetings-card verse that is so moving. Yes, you can laugh at
the ad's failings if you must. But its expression of an urgent
search for a formal and ritual mode of address — even in an
intimate letter to the writer's own mother — is touching precisely
because it suggests that prose is inadequate to such a task. There
is a modest daring in ordinary people's recourse to verse at such
times that, we seem collectively agreed, is appropriate and
honourable.

My opening attack on the quality of the verse in this
collection, therefore, may be irrelevant to the ultimate success
of the venture. I don't for a moment retract my opinion that the
book contains a lot of bad poetry; but it also makes a number of
strong, emotional statements of a kind which have been censored
out of press accounts of the epidemic. The very fact that a political
figure like Peter Tatchell has contributed a poem to the book
strikes me as indicative of its commitment, not only to the causes
with which people like him are so strongly associated, but also
to the idea that all modes of communication should be opened to
the needs of people with AIDS and their friends. How can you
write a poem when you're dying of AIDS? Well, how can you not?

BEAUTIFUL VEINS

Hervé Guibert, *To the Friend Who Did Not Save My Life* (London: Quartet, 1991), *The Compassion Protocol* (London: Quartet, 1993), *The Man in the Red Hat* (London: Quartet, 1993) and *Le Paradis* (Paris: Gallimard, 1992)

Regardless of its effect on their bodies, AIDS has had a variety of effects on the work of the writers who have had to live with it. Some it silences, others it inspires. In the case of Hervé Guibert, it prompted several books in quick succession, speed being more or less essential in HIV's unpredictable universe. Moreover, his illness having burdened even the most minor events in his daily existence with the duty of signification, it gave him the confidence to fictionalise his own journals. If it is true that his books tend to teeter on a line between failure and success, the chances of their succeeding depend on the apotheosis of the mundane.

In one of his late journals, posthumously published under the title *Cytomégalovirus*, Guibert remarked that in the old days people used to say he had beautiful lips, or eyes, but that now, well into the development of his illness, nurses only ever said he had beautiful veins. This displacement in the perception of his physique from aesthetic or erotic appreciation to the brisk pragmatism of the hospital ward may offer us a useful model of how the functions of his writing were eventually pared down. These are ugly books but they have beautiful veins.

A l'ami qui ne m'a pas sauvé la vie (To the Friend Who Did Not Save My Life) is best known for its portrayal of the character Muzil, based on Guibert's close friend Michel Foucault, in the last weeks of his life. The book is, in effect, an account of how AIDS dawned on the Parisian intellectual community, from first rumours of a gay cancer in 1980, through the elaborate mythologies of curiosity and ignorance, to the 'full-blown' epidemic itself. In an interim of alternating euphoria and depression, the syndrome moved from the mind to the individual thinker's body — or rather, in the case of Muzil/Foucault, from his intellect to his brain. Oddly enough, however, Guibert tends to continue to deal with his own illness as if it were a perplexing idea.

Much of his fiction about living with AIDS is as dry and unsentimental as you could imagine, a far cry from most of the

books one is used to from the United States. Indeed, it is possible
to consume many pages of Guibert and remain unmoved. It may
be that he succeeds too well in conveying the sheer dullness of
living with a condition which, although so often dramatised and
demonised by the press, is in fact, or can be, extremely slowly
degenerative; indeed, boring. It is really only in *Le Protocole
Compassionel (The Compassion Protocol)*, the central volume of
a trilogy — if that word does not suggest a structural progression
far more orderly than the three books really deliver — that
Guibert manages to convey through sustained novelistic scenes
an impression of the sheer extremity of AIDS as an existential
condition.

In this second book he covers the period of his hopeful
survival on a new drug, DDI, which a friend stole for him from
the bedside of a boy who had just died. Such are the subterfuges
which people with AIDS are driven to adopt by the sluggishness
of the drug companies' experimental protocols. While the French
press are prematurely referring to him as 'this dying man',
Guibert endures a quality of life which, despite his relative wealth
and his influential connections in the spheres of both culture and
health care, veers unpredictably between long weeks of tedium
and moments of extraordinary drama.

Among the latter are events which are all the more affecting
for the distance they establish between the patient, whose life
and sanity are at stake, and his doctors and nurses, to whom
they merely involve repetitions of routine tasks. An inhumanely
performed fibroscopy, described in horrific detail, sounds as if it
should fall within the remit of Amnesty International. Yet a
much more considerately performed alveolar lavage is appallingly
painful even so.

Other key moments deliver not so much the body as the
emotions into pain and risk, as when Guibert gets locked in the
cellar of his own apartment block and imagines, of all ironies,
that he may pre-empt his illness by dying there of starvation.
Later, in north Africa, a young man who, when he was twelve,
was a lover of Guibert's, now asks to see the writer's body again.
Guibert, who has been wasting away for months, agrees only if
the other, too, will undress. The sexual event which follows is
dehumanising and yet life-enhancing: an affront to a physique
still available to be affronted. Interrupting the even, understated
progress of the narrative, such episodes are genuinely
astonishing.

By contrast, *L'Homme au chapeau rouge (The Man in the Red Hat)* is a dull affair, rather aimlessly focused on art dealers and forgeries. For all his knowledge of the topic, Guibert says little of interest about the visual arts and gets low mileage out of the characters he introduces. His portrayal of the Greek painter Yannis Tsarouchis is particularly disappointing, since it says little about his personality and even less about his paintings. It is at this stage that the powers of the novelist seem to falter, giving way to those of the mundane diarist.

When the palimpsest of fiction and 'real' life is at its most transparent — which is to say, least fictional — it can result in passages of mere worldly gossip, such as the following: 'When I asked the ballet dancer Nureyev if I could interview him, I was eighteen, and he asked me straight out if I did brute sex, certainly I could but I told him the opposite, I never got my interview'. One does not need the first name of anyone as famous as Nureyev, but Guibert gets his revenge for the lost interview by distinguishing between the ballet dancer and any other Nureyevs who might have been in Paris at the time. The gossip itself is interesting enough, but what it is doing here is less certain. Even that almost surreptitious 'certainly I could' seems gratuitous.

Le Paradis, Guibert's last work before his death and more clearly a novel than its predecessors, begins in Martinique with the violent accidental death of the narrator's female lover, and then flashes back to the moment when their sex life reached its climax in the substitution of the woman's pistol for her lover's penis. The dead woman's passport is missing; indeed, the police establish that, under her only known name, 'Jayne Heinz', she never existed. Even the cassettes which she and the narrator used to listen to are found, after all, to be blank.

However, what starts in this manner as some kind of erotic thriller, posited on a mystery concerning identity and a death, soon becomes a much less amenable text. Just as its setting changes from the Caribbean holiday paradise of the title to the inhospitable terrain of central Africa, so too does the book itself become increasingly stark and uncomfortable, leaving the reader feeling displaced and without authority. The expected thriller is to the actual novel what the touristic Caribbean is to Guibert's Africa. Cast out of the paradise of a comfortable read, one is compelled to make other arrangements.

The point is, of course, that you will find a serpent in any paradise. Or if not a serpent, a bacillus at least. So insistent is

Guibert's characterisation of the world as a breeding ground for disease that, if one did not give him any credit for irony, his narrative might seem to evince the commonplace paranoia of the western traveller. A hotel shower is described as emitting 'un mince filet d'eau tiède, riche en microbes'. The travellers go equipped with a medicine box containing tranquilisers, antibiotics and, of course, Imodium for the treatment of diarrhoea. It is as a consequence of this fear of ill health that the very name of Mali mutates into the epithet 'ce pays de malheur'.

This is far from the pastoral north Africa which released André Gide into his love of boys. Guibert is conscious — perhaps rather archly self-conscious — of literary precedent here. It is not Gide to whom he refers, though, but two other figures from the gay canon, Arthur Rimbaud and Raymond Roussel. In the case of Rimbaud, the mystery of Africa lies not so much in the fact that it heterosexualised him (the converse of Gide) but that it was the place in which he became an adult — even, perhaps, a bit of a bourgeois. This was a transformative miracle indeed. Africa was the place where the anarchistic, homosexual, adolescent poet ceased to exist as such; a kind of empty quarter into which he vanished.

This sense of void is what enabled Raymond Roussel to write *Impressions d'Afrique* (1910) by projecting his imagination on to the reputation of the place rather than by actually going there. In terms of the old cliché, Roussel was more of a traveller than an arriver. When Guibert's narrator says he read Roussel before flying to Mali, 'pour retrouver l'odeur et la couleur de l'Afrique', one sees that *Le Paradis,* too, is intended less as a travel journal than as a fiction. After all, it has a heterosexual narrator who has tested HIV-negative but is called Hervé Guibert.

On the closing page, Guibert claims to have been taught nothing about Africa by either Rimbaud or Roussel: for, he says, 'je vois bien que l'Afrique n'existe pas'. Tell that to the Africans. The fact is that the phantom of the 'dark' continent is profoundly troubling to post-colonial French culture. For all his lofty decisiveness about Africa's very existence, Guibert appears to be as scared of the place itself as he is of the diseases he might contract there. By a useful irony, *L'homme au chapeau rouge* was to have ended with an account of a trip to Mali which Guibert made when already ill with the effects of AIDS and therefore vulnerable to opportunistic infection. However, that part of the manuscript went missing — or so he claims — and the book simply ends with a note to that effect.

Africa thus becomes a kind of postmodern black hole, a black
joke which absorbs experience to the point at which neither the
experience of entry nor the hole itself can be proved to have
existed. It imposes premature endings. Inevitably, one is led back
to one of the original myths of the etiology of AIDS — which
Guibert appears to endorse in *A l'ami qui ne m'a pas sauvé la
vie* — namely, that it spread to human society from green
monkeys in Africa. Within this mythology, Africa evokes the fear
not only of the other, but of the other bearing death. Africa is
an equivalent to the gay man in the tabloids, willfully spreading
disease.

When Cyril Collard's film *Les Nuits Fauves* opened in this
country recently, virtually every review mentioned the director's
death 'of AIDS', as if to confer on the film some kind of Leavisite
authenticity which it would not otherwise have had. The
gratuitous cachet of premature mortality gives publishers and
publicists an instant helping of 'poignancy' to exploit. The
supposition appears to be that fiction — even fiction about
'difficult' issues and 'serious' topics — has insufficient purchase
on its consumers to persuade them that its phantoms are truly
worthy of their emotions. Well, Guibert is dead too. If that is a
recommendation, let it recommend his books. Otherwise, let them
do so for themselves.

Hervé Guibert, *My Parents* (London: Serpent's Tail, 1993)

A simple book, this, but difficult to describe. In a characteristic
fusion of fiction and autobiography, Guibert gives an account of
his childhood from the implicit — and very distant — viewpoint
of what he knew was likely to be nearly the end of his life. Living
with AIDS, however, rather than coping with the common
illnesses of old age, he was still far nearer his youth than is
comfortable in this kind of valedictory retrospective.

Explicitly dedicated 'to nobody', *My Parents* is nevertheless
a tribute to a routinely difficult, suburban, bourgeois family in
the fifties and sixties, and to the kind of hit-and-miss upbringing
which somehow, unexpectedly, results in the adulthood of a
famous writer. There is manifest dedication to his parents in
every awkward scene.

The narrative has at least as much to do with bodies as with
minds. Yet the physical presence of his parents as sexual beings
is more psychologically than physically threatening to the boy.

To know (or believe) that one's father performed his own tonsilectomy with a sharp instrument and a hand-held mirror is to have to come to terms not only with physical courage, but also with extreme eccentricity (not to mention meanness).

All kinds of Oedipal risk are raised by the very lay-out of the family home, where certain rooms have to be crossed before others can be entered, certain doors are not provided with keys (or others are found unexpectedly locked) and paper-thin walls threaten to betray any but the most circumspect nocturnal activities.

Guibert can date exactly the moment when his love for his father turned into unwarranted hatred. Having arrived home early from school and interrupted his parents' love-making, the boy deliberately tracks down their used condom and runs his fingers through its stickiness. He narrates such incidents with a quiet intensity which never lapses into the self-dramatization that a lesser writer would rely on to achieve an arresting effect.

The process of writing sets Guibert at a certain distance — perhaps not far enough to be clinical — from himself, and at one point he happily shifts into the third person in order to estrange us from a boy with whom we have already become quite intimately familiar. To that extent, the book is like something by Christopher Isherwood, only less narcissistic, less smug. Indeed, the shift into the third person is altogether less shifty.

But it is Marcel Proust who really overshadows Guibert's text. In French literature, any gay man's account of his relationship with his parents, particularly with his mother, particularly if she ever (as here) refuses him a kiss, is vulnerable to damaging comparison with Proust. It is a mark of Guibert's achievement in *My Parents* that he survives the comparison intact. Indeed, Proust's *Swann's Way* would not be disgraced to sit on the same shelf.

SWEETLY UNSAVOURY

Edmund White, *Genet* (London: Faber, 1993)

After almost 600 pages of this monumental narrative, Edmund
White parenthetically and gratuitously exclaims, with all the
delight of a biographer who feels he has discovered the perfect
subject, 'Genet always seemed to appear at the right place at the
right time'. Three characteristic right places were Paris, Chicago
and Beirut; and their respective right times were 14 June 1940,
when Nazi troops entered the French capital, the 1968
Democratic Convention, and the 1982 Shatila massacre. These
coincidences of Genet's life with major international events have
offered White the opportunity to make a major contribution to
our understanding of modern culture. It is an opportunity he
takes up with cheerful efficiency.

Of course, Genet was also frequently apprehended in the
wrong place at the wrong time: on a train without a valid ticket,
outside a bookstore with a stolen book in his pocket, hundreds
of miles from the regiment he was supposed to be serving in. His
opinions, too, could be conspicuously out of step with the moment
in which he expressed them. As late as 1977 he was dismissive
of Stalin's atrocities. He never moved far in his insensitivity to
all female roles but that of the dignified and long-suffering
mother. His attitudes to homosexuality began to seem
particularly archaic in the decade after Gay Liberation.

The crimes are many, but they turn out to have been far
more trivial than merited his subsequent reputation. They
impress, if at all, by cumulative effect rather than by establishing
much depth of moral perversity. Unlike the murderers in his
novels, he was a thief and a thug, an inefficient shop-lifter and
a cowardly mugger of elderly homosexual men. Nothing in his
life merits either his reputation for evil or the consequent
beatification he received at the hands of Jean-Paul Sartre. To
that extent, he was an ordinary mortal.

Born in 1910 to a single mother who soon abandoned him
into care, Jean Genet was raised by foster parents in the village
of Alligny-en-Morvan. He received only seven years of formal
primary education before being put to work as a farm hand at
the age of thirteen. Repeated petty thefts and attempts to run
away resulted in his being sent, in 1926, to the 'children's prison'

at Mettray, where his moderate beauty and willing passivity gave him a certain protected value and sowed the imaginative seeds of what would later become a book called *Miracle of the Rose*. No great patriot, Genet joined the army in 1929 as a way of escaping Mettray. But although service life gave him the opportunity to travel — a tour of duty to Syria persuaded him of the justice of the Arab nationalist cause — he was unable to submit to authority for long. He did sign up for further tours of duty but eventually, in 1936, he deserted and spent a year travelling around Europe on a false passport. On his return to France he was discharged by the military for reasons of mental instability and sexual deviation.

After a series of arrests for minor crimes, Genet was sent to prison for three months at the end of 1941. By the time he re-emerged — by some miracle which Edmund White never quite manages to pin down — he had become a writer: he had started *Our Lady of the Flowers*. Jean Cocteau read the manuscript and set about trying to get it published. His encouragement was instrumental in the fact that Genet wrote four more novels in the next three years; but being championed by the Parisian intelligentsia led just as surely to his subsequent silence. Cocteau and Sartre managed to arrange an apparently unnecessary and irregular Presidential pardon for the increasingly famous writer-thief, but when Sartre published the massive *Saint Genet* in 1952, Genet destroyed five years' worth of his own manuscripts. He never wrote fiction again. It was as a dramatist that he next allowed his voice to be heard, during a spurt of activity in 1955 and 1956. After the 1964 suicide of his lover Abdallah, a circus acrobat, he destroyed another large batch of papers and renounced literature, again, for good. This renunciation, too, came unstuck when, in his final years, he put together *Prisoner of Love* at the request of Yasser Arafat.

Though unheroic, some of his crimes were literally inspiring: they formed the basis of the cultural education he would otherwise have been denied by his early life under the *Assistance Publique* and in the penal colony at Mettray. He tore his favourite Baudelaire poems out of a borrowed copy of *Les Fleurs du Mal,* thereby confirming what was to prove a lifelong faith in mutilation as an act of homage. Having once read the first sentence of Marcel Proust's *Within a Budding Grove,* he stole the rest of *Remembrance of Things Past* volume by volume. Although he was temperamentally closer to Arthur Rimbaud, it was in reading Proust that he learned a skill which is easier to name than to master: the art of the long sentence.

Whether we need the biography of an autobiographical writer is always open to question, if only momentarily and for trivial reasons. Certain classic examples, such as Richard Ellmann's life of James Joyce, appear to settle the issue. We need the biography to the extent that we wish to evaluate the scope of the autobiography's lies. The biography becomes a measure of the fiction's fictionality — which is precisely why Genet was hostile to biographers and biographical interviewers. Their aim was to unmask the literal facts behind his own 'poetic' (which might be to say 'distorted') truths. He demanded the right to allow his falsehoods to seep into the record of the truth and remain there. Unlike most liars, he wanted to seem less virtuous than he really was. He exaggerated the suffering of his childhood, and then exaggerated the extent of his criminality. It was never his aim as a writer simply to record quotidian events. Perhaps the oddest of many odd moments in Genet's underrated last book, *Prisoner of Love*, occurs when he forgets his own career to the extent of naively asking, 'But what if it were true that writing is a lie?'

It may be that, in this particular case, some of us need a biography to justify our reading the books of a crook. Perhaps, too, there are still those who need to be spoon-fed reasons for reading the books of a sodomite. Certainly, it is as well to be reminded of how far Sartre's *Saint Genet* was effective in establishing Genet's reputation as a serious writer. White has many reservations about that version of the life, and usefully corrects it on a number of occasions. But each book has its distinctive character and value. On balance, the Sartre is probably more searching on the question of theft; the White is certainly more rational on the sexuality.

Edmund White never bothers trying to justify his enterprise; nor should he. The vigour of his narrative and the accumulation of revealing detail, in the end, speak for themselves. Of course, one should grant White the dignity of an intertextual progression here. The logic of his own career leads triumphantly into this book, one gay writer's breathless homage to an illustrious predecessor. For lack of procreative genealogies, homosexual writers view literary influences with the utmost seriousness. In a sense, White is laying claim, through Genet, to the paternity of Proust. In order to do so, he has to persuade himself and us that an invert and a homosexual and a gay man all belong to the same family, albeit to successive generations.

However, in some respects this eagerness allows White to gloss over the awkward faultlines in homosexual history. For instance, it is all very well to say that André Gide's *Corydon* is 'a faintly ridiculous defence of homosexuality' — indeed, some might say it is *extremely* ridiculous — but it seems churlish not to have added that what now seems ridiculous required massive resources of both intellect and courage in the ridiculous era of its composition. By thus trivialising or skimming over major documents in the modern history of sexuality, White leaves himself unprepared for some of the more problematic issues which Genet's writing raises. A major question arises, not just in the semantics, but in relation to our whole conceptual understanding of men who have sex with other men, when White allows a glib paradox to sum up a central issue. *Querelle of Brest,* he says, is 'a novel about homosexuality in which none of the characters is homosexual'. More attention to both Proust and Gide on the thorny question of the etiology of homosexuality, and to current debates around nature and nurture, might have persuaded White to take greater care. Certainly, when he offers a summary of French 'gay novels' published in 1953, one begins to wonder if he has decided to override the niceties of linguistic chronology. His use of the English word 'pederast' as a translation of its French twin is similarly flawed.

Language is, after all, the crux of Jean Genet's claim to literary value. While his texts do contain dramatic events — murders, betrayals, sexual collisions — the bulk of the drama is generated by in the astonishing way in which he describes them and the effect of his imagination upon their subsequent existence. It has been said before and may now sound banal, but language is his main protagonist. Language establishes his purchase on whatever one means by 'the truth'.

True or not, one can always argue with his brutal maxims. For instance, when he claims, in *Prisoner of Love,* that 'Anyone who hasn't experienced the ecstasy of betrayal knows nothing about ecstasy at all', one might prosaically object that anyone who hasn't experienced the pain of having been betrayed knows nothing about betrayal at all. However, this gets us nowhere. It is a bit like protesting to Oscar Wilde, 'But each man *loves* the thing he loves!' Thus to state the obvious within the cult and culture of the paradox is to prove oneself bourgeois and, worse still, heterosexual. Something of the sort occurs in *Saint Genet,* when Sartre rhetorically and magnanimously proclaims that *'Man* is a homosexual, a thief and a traitor'. As if immediately losing his nerve, he adds a footnote allowing that 'He is *also,* of course, heterosexual, honest and faithful'. A half-hearted paradox invariably exposes itself as humbug.

Like Wilde, Genet felt that his relationship with language was profoundly affected by his sexuality. In his view, homosexual writers could not simply use language in a straightforward manner as a transparent medium. They were forced to comment on it — 'alter it, parody it, dissolve it' — from a marginal position at a fixed distance. The literature of homosexuality was, therefore, stigmatised with involuntary irony. Genet claimed to have discovered his own method and voice by accident. In 1939, in his late twenties, he wrote a belated Christmas card from jail. Instead of sending conventional greetings, he found himself commenting reflexively on the colour and texture of the card itself, the surface on which he was writing. Never again would he write an unselfconscious sentence.

Of course, this explains both the extraordinary rhetorical poise of his prose and its dangerously overwrought quality, forever risking absurdity. In a 1986 essay on Dostoevsky he argued that 'any novel, poem, painting, piece of music that doesn't set itself up as a shooting gallery in which it is one of the targets is a fake'. It is one of the points of art, not only to open itself to attack, but even to open the attack on itself. Hence the often irritatingly narcissistic strategies of even his most straightforward texts.

Besides himself, whom was Genet trying to impress? In the dandyism of the way he dressed, according to Sartre's secretary Jean Cau, 'It was obvious he was dressing up to impress the people of Pigalle, not Saint-Germain'. That is to say, he had his own constituency; he was not a snob with aspirations. However, when White calls him 'the Proust of marginal Paris', one has to add the rider that he was writing from and of the margins, but not for them. It was apparently a matter of regret to him that he could not write as he dressed — as it were, for Pigalle rather than Saint-Germain. As he once complained to one of his lovers — who seems to have been a case in point — 'None of the people I write about can understand my work'.

So he was left in the situation of having to address readers for whom he had varying degrees of contempt and who would automatically be shocked by things which he and his fellow convicts had taken for granted. Even so, he would have preferred a more shockable reader than closeted homosexual masturbators and their cerebral equivalents, the French intelligentsia. In conversation with Madeleine Gobeil, he lamented the fact that his publishers were targeting readers who 'knew what they were getting'. Like the bourgeois people whose homes he stayed in ('if I don't steal something from them they're not happy'), while buying his books such readers had already allowed for a certain degree of shock. He wished that *Our Lady of the Flowers* 'had fallen into the hands of Catholic bankers or into thatched cottages, or amongst policemen or *concierges*'. In that respect, his reputation as a pornographer was distinctly limiting. Although *Querelle of Brest* is explicitly 'addressed to inverts', Genet wanted to feel that hordes of unsuspecting heterosexuals would somehow end up eavesdropping on the address.

It was always easy to see whom he did not impress. His detractors tended to raise their voices when speaking out against him. Paul Valéry said *Our Lady of the Flowers* should be burned. Jean-Marie Le Pen was among the leaders of those who demonstrated against the 1966 production of *The Screens*. Ed Bullins argued that black Americans should not go to see *The Blacks* on the grounds that Genet was 'a white, self-confessed homosexual with dead white Western ideas — faggoty ideas about Black Art, Revolution, and people'. Clearly, Genet had anticipated, even invited, many of these attacks. Who can forget the wonderful moment when he affronted liberal opinion in the United States by admiring the thighs of the policemen who had so lustily broken up the yippie demonstrations at the 1968 Democratic Convention?

Although no one should doubt his belief in the power of poetry, Genet was demonstrative in his contempt for writing as a career. He claimed his main reason for writing books was to get out of prison; when he was free, he stopped. Later in life, he would write when he was running out of money. He also had the habit of persuading gullible publishers to pay for texts which he had no intention of writing at all. Even so, he never ceased asking for reassurance that his books were of lasting value. He clearly wanted to think himself capable of doing what Arthur Rimbaud had done before him — to write great works and then to disown them, together with the whole system of values which judged them great — but it seems he was reluctant to give up some of the privileges which came with great-writer status. Not the fame, from which he fled into an obsessive privacy in transient hotel rooms, but the access to money and to travel. To Genet, travel meant the ability to escape France. Whenever he absconded as a child, he was always apprehended on his way to a major port. Edmund White reminds us that his written works are often set overseas: *The Balcony* in Spain, *The Blacks* in Africa, *The Screens* in Algeria, and so on. Genet hated the French establishment for what it had done to him as a child. Although during the occupation he slept with German soldiers, he was no fascist; but he is on record as having been delighted when Hitler 'gave a thrashing to the French'. What mattered was the thrashing, not Hitler. He would have been just as pleased if the conqueror had been Winston Churchill or Judy Garland.

The main point about the biography of an autobiographer is that, if it works, it should send us back to the original texts. Edmund White's dignified and authoritative study cannot fail to do this. It reminds the reader, not only of Genet's claims to greatness, but also of all the arguments which have been marshalled against it. Although he loves Genet, White also seems to have loved re-reading his detractors. After all, it is the inevitability of a dialogue between two morally opposed world views that makes the experience of reading Genet such an engaged and engaging experience. His books are unsavoury to the extent of being very sweet indeed.